Unfolding Journeys:
Ways to Connect

The Universal Conscious Community

Published by OMNE Publishing in 2021

A catalogue record for this book is available from the National Library of Australia

Content Producer - International Energetic Healing Association (IEHA) www.internationaleha.org

Cover design and illustrations - Nastia Gladushchenko www.nastia-gladushchenko.com

Internal read proofing/ author mentoring - Jenny Fitzgerald www.jennyfitzgerald.com.au

Print layout and kindle by OMNE Publishing www.omne.com.au

Editing by Teresa Goudie

Project management - Irina Gladushchenko (IEHA)

Printed by OMNE Publishing

This book is available in print, Kindle and audiobook formats.

Dedication

We dedicate this book to all the humble life travellers who trust and are willing to connect with the light within to fully engage in their life journey.

Contents

Foreword

by Jane Woods

In the beginning we had one word. That word was love. With the same letters that make the word 'love', we can make the word 'evolve'. This is what we are doing when we allow active healing to take place within our beings. For some, it's not that easy; it's almost as if some of us were born with pre-ordered settings to make things difficult.

Why would this be so? I believe it is so that we may evolve as much as possible for our soul's benefit. I also believe we have life lessons to learn, and through these difficult circumstances we may find ourselves in, we are in a better position to learn those life lessons.

I am honoured to be the custodian of the "Unfolding Journeys: Ways to Connect" book. I thank you for taking the time to read, reflect upon and perhaps imbue the energy of the stories within. I hope that they may inspire, heal and entertain you.

With love, may you evolve.

"We are UNITED on the primary cosmic value of Love…
Engaging in my CREATIVE FLOW, I LOVE…"
~Irina Gladushchenko

Unfolding Journeys

The Power of Tuning In
by Martine Negro

*"When you walk your destiny through
your heart-mind, everything flows."*

~Martine Negro

The strongest connection with my inner guidance I have ever experienced came through so loudly it was impossible for me to dismiss it, even though it did not make any logical sense at the time. 20 years ago, I was spending a few months in Provence and was invited to a psycho-spiritual training in Paris by a lovely lady I met there. The teaching was well presented, and I enjoyed it, even though there was nothing new. Being the only participant from Australia, I was graciously offered the chance to move to the second level, free of charge. Having nothing to lose and looking forward to new learnings, I readily accepted. I was introduced to more lovely and friendly people and everything was flowing smoothly.

At the end of it, I was approached by one of the organisers. With great excitement he said, "Martine, you have enjoyed the first two levels of our course. Why not complete level three and join our organisation? That way you can take this training to Australia and represent us there!" I was caught by surprise and flattered, but at the same time the request did not feel right.

"Don't you think it is a bit rushed? My plane is leaving this afternoon!" I said.

"No problem! I can arrange the ceremony right now! I'll be back in five minutes," and he ran out of the room. I was now alone, confused, and feeling an uncomfortable tightness in my chest increasing in intensity every second. I now had four minutes left to decide whether to go ahead with the ceremony or not. I needed to know what to do quickly but did not have enough time to think. There was no other option than to tune in.

Respectfully, placing my hands on my chest, I humbly asked for guidance. Unexpectedly, and in an instant, I could hear every cell in my body screaming, "Get out now!" I could feel every cell shaking and amplifying the same crystal-clear message!

Inwardly, I thanked my body and took a few slow, deep breaths to re-center myself. The door opened and the same man, now dressed up in a white long robe, took me by the hand to a large hall at the back of the house filled with ten more people in white cloaks forming an open circle. He left me standing in the middle facing the Headmaster of what I now felt was a sect!

At the first opportunity, I declared my decision to go no further and to leave.

They allowed me to go! I left the building 'floating', like a bird leaving a cage! A memorable, still-vivid experience which reminds me to ask, trust and act on my inner wisdom.

The Phoenix
by Emma Taylor

"You've seen my descent.
Now watch my rising."

~RUMI

In one way or another we can all relate to the Greek myth of the phoenix, a mystical bird that sets itself on fire and rises from its own ashes. It's a story that resonates within us all because as humans we will experience at some point in time aspects of our life 'turning into ashes', whereby we have to rise to the challenge of adversity by facing the inevitable process of loss.

For me, life burst into flames on 20th October 2016 when, at age 31, I was diagnosed with an invasive breast cancer. I felt dirty. I felt guilty, as if I lacked inner purity and something was intrinsically wrong with me. I felt tainted. I felt like my body had betrayed me, as if my mind and body were two separate entities. It was this distorted illusion and disconnect that had in fact resulted in this dis-ease within me. I was disconnected from my core, unsure of who I was, where I wanted to be and was holding onto unresolved emotional debris and beliefs that I later realised were the root causes of the dis-ease. The tumors were a physical manifestation of such stagnation and were my body's way of signaling that energy was blocked and change needed to happen.

I endured five months of chemotherapy followed by a bilateral mastectomy, yet the whole time my main fear wasn't the loss of my life, but rather the loss of the life I had envisioned and the potential loss of my fertility. The chance to fall pregnant and birth my own baby was threatened by a significantly reduced egg count as a result of chemotherapy. IVF was the first obvious option; but was that the right path to take considering I was in a hyper-vigilant state of survival, with fear and anxiety being the driving force behind my decision?

As human beings we are hardwired to feel the need to control every aspect of our lives – we are conditioned to always be progressing, planning and striving in life. When we don't feel in control, fear can arise due to the illusion that control leads to safety. Yet what I discovered is that fear is in fact one of the greatest inhibitors to intuition, making it difficult to connect with our innate wisdom and trust.

Surrendering and letting go of control and allowing life to happen, which in my case meant accepting my low egg count due to the treatment I had chosen, and relinquishing my attachments to the future, wasn't easy. The universe sent me two special lightworkers to help me rise from the ashes. Natalie, a traditional Chinese doctor; and Valery, an energetic healer, both facilitated deep physical, emotional and spiritual healing within me.

Receiving acupuncture from Natalie twice a week during treatment helped build qi and vitality which provided support to counteract the onslaught of chemo. Feeling the powerful physical effects of acupuncture sparked a burning passion within me and is the reason why I am now a practicing kinesiologist and a mind and body medicine practitioner working with the meridian system. I am a walking, living, grateful advocate who continues to benefit from regular acupuncture to maintain optimal cellular health.

And then there was Valery; a universal light worker who facilitated great energetic healing within me, leading me down an alternate path to IVF. Valery helped me to reconnect with unresolved emotional trauma that had left my sacral and heart chakras misaligned and dense. He helped ignite a fire within, turning on a valve to allow warmth and light to enter into the sacred space of the uterus, the centre of creation, clearing out the old and laying the foundation for the new. By creating positive energy though conscious thought, word and behaviour, I was able to replace fear with hope and reconnect with an inner trust knowing that the universe would support me in whichever way the future was to unfold.

This experience of loss didn't happen TO me, but rather it happened FOR me. Like the phoenix that rose from the ashes, I too was reborn, renewed and transformed with an expanded awareness and more empowered connection and sense of self. I learned that loss is inevitable, but with grief the divine always presents greater opposing relief. The relief for me came in no greater reward than the gift of health and the privilege of motherhood.

Embracing Resilience
by Amy Morse

*"In every fork of life, twist and turn, hill or mountain,
the only way clear is to pursue life with passion and
desire. In the end it will be so worth it."*

~Amy Morse

When I was 19, I moved to Sydney and met a man at my cousin's wedding. Soon after we developed a relationship and moved in together. We were very surprised by my pregnancy and, when I was 20, I gave birth to my son Jonathan. Having a baby is difficult at the best of times, and I was young, and the relationship didn't work out. By the time my son was one year old I was a single mother.

Life was tough! Moving out meant finding a place of my own on a very tight budget. My parents lived out of Sydney, so I had limited support. I scraped together enough furniture and set up a one bedroom flat. I had an old car that required me to tap the starter motor in the cold early mornings to get it going. It may seem ridiculous but during the time of my relationship breakdown and setting up a new life with a child, I enrolled in a university degree to achieve my goal of becoming a Registered Nurse.

My relationship with my ex-partner was volatile and, although he cared for Jonathan on alternate weekends, there was ongoing bitterness and resentment between us. It took a lot of determination to fulfil my role as a mother and complete a university degree, as well as working part-time to supplement the government pension I received. It was exhausting and I recall suffering extreme insomnia at times and was often anxious. It was a tough road!

Being on my own at such a young age with the responsibility of a child made things real for me. It made me strive harder for a better future. It gave me strong will and determination to never give up.

At 25 years old I proudly wore the academic gown and hat and graduated with a credit. I was a Registered Nurse! What an amazing four years it had been. It was such a proud moment!

What I have learned is to never give up on your dreams. Everything in life is possible if you work hard to achieve your goals, no matter how difficult it may seem at the time. Reaching towards the finish line can see us swimming to the top, emerging into magical crystal-clear water, opening our eyes as we breathe in the fresh air and feelings of achievement, the silver lining of surviving hardship and resilience. When our hearts embrace success our eyes open to a radiant blue sky and warm yellow sunshine making it all worthwhile. It's through the hard times that we are given an opportunity to turn things around for the better.

I'm 40 now, and I continue to work as a nurse in community nursing.

My son has turned out to be amazing; life is good!

Collaboration over Competition

by Nastia Gladushchenko

*"By finishing each other's works, we relinquish control
and allow the work to evolve and grow in a new way
according to its new environment, just like a plant."*

~Nastia Gladushchenko

This is a story about learning to understand yourself and all life around you through collaboration.

As a painter and mural artist inspired by plants, I often work independently to create and understand the world in my own way; but I do also love a challenge. So, when a fellow botanical artist approached me and suggested we make one or two pieces together by finishing each other's work, I was intrigued and accepted to take part in this experiment.

When one day the postman dropped off eight pieces, I felt a little overwhelmed because it felt like a much bigger project than I had expected, and my first reaction was to run. I sat with the works in my studio for a couple of weeks before I could bring myself to touch them. Just looking at them gave me anxiety because I had never dared to paint over someone else's work before. The work was already beautiful: lush, full of patterns, colours and layered shapes and I couldn't see a way to bring my style in.

With an exhibition scheduled only a month away to show this body of collaborative work in a gallery in Sydney, I decided to start with very small gestures on one small piece because I was running out of time. Making my marks on the piece, I was surprised at how well our two styles were talking to each other, so I shared a quick photograph with my collaborator and, after a nervous wait, I finally received a response. She loved it! Far out, what a relief.

After these slow initial steps, we ended up messaging and calling each other daily to check in on one another's work and life, and this supportive exchange became vital to our collaboration. We realised that we were making art with the same adaptability, fluidity and cohesion that plants need to grow and survive, accidentally mimicking our subject matter. Our two very different styles and approaches to painting were starting to balance each other and we began to understand how the other thought and worked. Giving my pieces away to be finished by another artist was liberating and fun because we had built trust and I knew the pieces would be re-invented and worked on with love. It was a month of opening 'gifts' from each other as we sent work back and forth between our studios in Sydney and the Blue Mountains. We loved this process more than we ever expected to and 'collaboration over competition' became our mantra.

With the pieces coming together ahead of time, we saw them forming a strong and unified body of work that we were proud of despite, and perhaps because of, its experimental nature. Both our collectors and followers were intrigued by this process too and the fact that these 20 or so pieces would be completely unique and painted by two artists brought a real sense of excitement to the show.

We knew we were onto something really interesting when we started the project and despite the challenges, the outcome and the response to the work made for a truly positive and rich experience. Thanks to this experiment, we formed a special bond and connection over our love of plants and each other's work.

The Creative Block
by Eva Tiborcz (Tcz.) Sterlich

"Upon a branch of nothingness
my heart sits trembling voicelessly,
and watching, watching, numberless,
the mild stars gather round to see."

~Attila József

I come from a large, traditional Hungarian/German family. Education and good manners were priorities, so my upbringing was strict and disciplined. I was surrounded by musicians, painters, architects, doctors, teachers, industrial developers, and designers as I was growing up.

My father's hobby was painting. He would paint magical landscapes. I asked him once, "Where are these places?" He replied, "They come from my soul."

The poem by Attila József, above, was introduced to me when I was 13 years old. It touched me to the core and has stayed with me all in my life. It had a huge impact on me. The following year my father died, and this poem became an intuitive alarm for when a crisis was about to happen. It would come to my mind and I would know to be aware.

When I was 16, I had to choose my career. I became an educator and a painter because I love knowledge as well as the visual arts.

As an artist I have experienced many creative blocks. A creative block can be very disturbing. I experience it as falling into a black hole, where all my values are baseless, nothing can be known or communicated, I believe in nothing, and have no purpose other than perhaps an impulse to destroy. The block impacts all areas of my life. It affects my mental and emotional states; it affects my routines; it creates an inability to progress; I feel overwhelmed and personal problems are intensified.

Occasionally I lose momentum altogether which means the work has to be put aside and I do something completely different until the time is right for the project.

Step by step, I manage to navigate myself out of these states with the help of people around me as well as my intuition. I have learned to ask questions in each of the areas that the block manifests so I can move forward again. There isn't a one size fits all to clearing the creative block. It's a matter of navigating until something works or is revealed to me. Here are a few things that I try....

I ask, "What if...?" and try out different perspectives. I expose myself to different experiences and activities besides making art, and I travel to learn from other cultures. I face the unknown, which can be scary, especially when something is revealed about me that I have been hiding such as fear, pain, insecurity, or loneliness. I begin experimenting with different mediums and new materials, always looking for new possibilities and techniques. Sometimes I have to go back to basics, making lots of studies with different mediums. I keep working at it until I find what 'feels right'.

Creative blocks can be paralysing but what I know is they are not confined to an artist's work; they occur for everyone. There is no light without the shade and all the blocks we experience have a purpose – to MAKE a person.

Darkness to Light
by Jenny Fitzgerald

"The best way out is always through."

~Robert Frost

She knew instinctively how to keep herself safe in her dysfunctional family where arguments, intolerance and hate were the norm. Every Sunday she would walk for miles to sit in the church and listen, sing and just be…even though she had no idea what they were talking about, she loved the way she felt when she was there. It was her connection and it helped her deal with life at home.

She grew up, got married and life was wonderful and easy. Then, on a day just like any other, for no reason she can remember, she suddenly became terrified of everything. It began with a fear that she might choke on the skins of fruits and vegetables and progressed over time to a full-blown Obsessive Compulsive Disorder.

Her life became a hell on earth! For the first five years she didn't know what to do, and she became more and more unwell. She had more horrific thoughts, each one worse than the last, until she became terrified that she might kill her children. Depression descended upon her and she could no longer feel the love she had always trusted. She was lost and alone.

She was terrified of losing control and finally confessed to her doctor that she was scared she might kill her children. The doctor asked, "Do you want to kill them?" This was the most extraordinary question she had ever been asked, and she replied, "NO! Of course not!" Recognising what was wrong, the doctor referred her to a psychiatrist who told her she had Obsessive Compulsive Disorder and would need to take anti-depressants for the rest of her life.

That was the best shock treatment she could have hoped for, because she didn't believe drugs were an answer to anything. Mental health was what she wanted; not to be drugged out.

Thus began her quest for mental health.

She went to many practitioners. Nothing seemed to be working. She was still terrified and seriously depressed. An opportunity to go to a spiritual church opened a new door. A psychic at that church told her that her grandmother was with her and that she would be okay; that she would rise above this dark night of the soul and would be victorious.

Not long after this she was offered a place in a weekend workshop. It was a personal development workshop and that was all she knew about it, but she just knew she had to go. Some of her work colleagues were going too, so she thought it would be a safe experience.

Over the course of the weekend she learned and experienced the miracle of going within and finding the TRUTH. She learned that every experience she ever had, had impacted her, and that she had the power to heal. For the first time in ten years she felt what it was like to be free from anxiety. It only lasted 36 hours, but it was a glimmer of hope that she could attain peace again.

She became like a dog with a bone. Every day, pretty much as often as she could, she used the technique she'd learned to travel into the depths of her self and find the TRUTH. She learned that no one had done anything to her, it was the perception she had created to make sense of the events and experiences she had.

This simple process of forgiveness became her life's work.

The transformation didn't happen in an instant; it unfolded over time, but this was the answer to a life of peace and tranquility beyond anything she could ever have imagined. And it was the beginning of her deep spiritual connection that grows deeper every day.

Healing for Younger Self

by Izumi Amauchi

"Music and rhythm find their way
into the secret places of the SOUL."

-Plato

"For my beautiful son,
Tohma and my younger SELF.
Life is full of miracles."

-Izumi Amauchi

Last year, when my eight-year-old son asked me to take him for a piano lesson trial, my first reaction was, "Oh, no!"

For over 40 years, I had managed to avoid facing the self-limiting belief that I was incompetent and too stupid to play music. I believed it so strongly that I thought I must have significant learning difficulties around reading music. Now my son wanted to take lessons so I decided to face my demons. I wanted to have a healthy, positive attitude towards learning music for his sake.

Because I guide people using a technique called 'Matrix Reimprinting' to change limiting beliefs, I knew I could change the beliefs I had formed at an early age. I had erased my memories from a time passed, and the Pandora's box had never been opened until my beautiful son decided he wanted to play the piano.

I started to tune in to my feelings and chased memories to reach my core memory. As the clouds began to clear I saw my younger, seven-year-old self on a stage with three other children. It was my first electric piano concert. We were about to start playing. I sensed that my younger self was feeling helpless and ashamed of herself. What was she ashamed of? She switched off her electric piano and pretended to play. It was the only way to stop anyone from finding out that she did not know how to play. She had never enjoyed going to the lessons. No matter how much time and effort her mother put in to teach her how to read the music notes, they did not register. She was mortified about her inability to learn music. Soon after the concert, she quit piano. The shameful event at the concert haunted her profoundly.

As I talked to my younger self I found out that instead of being paralysed by the fear of getting into trouble for not knowing how to read music and play, she wanted to talk to someone about it, then find a way to practice until she felt safe to play on the stage.

I created a scene with her. I told her, "It is okay, you know, you are so young. You couldn't tell your feelings to your piano teacher nor your mum. I am here to help you. Let's do it together. I stand by you. You are a good girl. You are doing this to enjoy the music, not for competition or beating yourself."

I changed my belief to I am good / I am creative. The harmonious flow of musical tunes filled my body and expanded to all my energy fields. All my senses were awakening. My soul was touched by rhythm.

Learning how to play the piano with my son has been truly liberating.

This is the truth about life. When we are in alignment with sheer joy without any expectation, we are in a divine place. The most beautiful thing is that I was present when my son proudly played a piano solo on the stage of a beautiful serene church last year for his very first piano concert. I was watching him with sheer joy and triumph. My younger self was beaming with joy!

This has been a miracle in my life, and I know it has opened me up to a higher vibrational realm.

Life Goes on

by Corinne Dosoruth

"Wildflower; pick up your pretty little head,
It will get easier, your dreams are not dead."

-Nikki Rowe

I come from Mauritius, an island in the Indian Ocean. It was successively settled by the Arabs, Portuguese, Dutch, French and British until it attained independence in 1968. Aside from European settlers, it was also inhabited by African, Indian, Chinese and Pakistani workers; hence its very multicultural make-up.

It was only a matter of time before mixed marriages started. My ancestors are a mixture of French and African. We are called Creoles. Creoles had a lot of rituals, probably inherited from Africa. From an early age I remember witnessing some of these. I once saw my grandmother placing a butter knife in the soil and dropping salt all around it and asking for a major cyclone that was heading our way to pass so that my aunty could get married that day. The storm did pass, and the sun shone brightly.

Rituals, superstitions, and spells are quite common across Mauritian folklore. My dad used to say, "Always honour your ancestors." He built a cement table where, every Friday, he would pray to his parents who had died. He believed all the blessings he received over the years came from them.

My dad died 18 years ago and that was my first glimpse of another world, realm or place – whichever you want to call it – where life goes on. I wasn't able to travel to his funeral and his spirit 'came' all the way here to say goodbye. For a week afterwards, I felt his presence everywhere in my house. In my dreams he would tell me he was okay but the place he was in was hot. He gave me information, such as my sister's upcoming wedding date, and he also told me I would have a child and it would be a boy.

My grandmother died a couple of years later when I was trying desperately to fall pregnant. She also came to visit me in a dream and showed me this little boy in her arms while my mum and all my sisters were standing next to me. After this I received several messages from my aunty who also died.

Now, I am more aware of when there are spirits in my house. I have caught glimpses of tall angels, white lights, and also dark and scary lights. I have had nightmares about bad things too. The week my father-in-law died in February 2020, my house was full of spirits and it felt like they were hanging around, waiting for something. The day he died my house went back to its normal self.

After reading, studying and researching the afterlife, I now know that there is life after death and that our ancestors are looking after us and giving us small or big blessings if we also keep looking after them when they pass. Years after my first experience of seeing the rituals my family performed, I find myself doing the same rituals.

My message is to always be aware, look for signs, feelings, strange noises… they warn you of dangers but also send you messages of hope and love. They are here around us. We just have to open our eyes and hearts to see them.

She Listens Still

by Maxine Pagliasso

*"When a precious family member passes, it's comforting
to know that they are still there.
But sometimes, they turn up in the most unexpected
places and in the most beautiful forms."*

\- Maxine Pagliasso

The last five years of my Nanna's life was spent indoors, like a prisoner, because she suffered from agoraphobia. So, when I announced my wedding date and asked her if she would be attending, I already knew what her reply would be. The reply didn't matter because I had devised a plan that was guaranteed to make my Nanna smile. I planned to visit her on my wedding day, on the way to the church. If Nanna was unable to come to the wedding to see the bride get married, then the bride would come to her. We would hug, have photos taken and memories would be made. More importantly, I wanted to see her smile.

But even the most well-devised plans don't always work out. Nanna passed away exactly one week before the wedding. As devastating as her passing was, there was also a part of me that took comfort in knowing that she would bear witness to the entire wedding now, from another dimension, far away yet very near.

Her death left a hole in my heart. She was like my second mum and the first close relative I had lost in my life. I'm not entirely sure how I managed to get through that week!

We buried Nanna and three days later, I was married. Despite the immense sadness, I felt a strange sense of peace. I continued to smile and was excited about my wedding day. I could feel Nanna near me and sensed she didn't want her passing to spoil my special day.

Two months later, I was pregnant, and we were living in Sydney's inner west. One morning, I awoke suddenly from a terrible dream. In the dream, I saw a big, ugly, grey building. It was about eight storeys high, with rows of tiny windows that had bars on them. It resembled a gaol. On the top floor, I saw my Nanna looking out of one of the windows, searching for something.

I began to cry. So many questions were running through my head. "Is Nanna trapped somewhere?" "Is she unhappy?" "What is she trying to communicate?" I was deeply concerned by the dream, but I needed to get to work.

Making my way to the train station, I was thinking about the dream and wondering why I had dreamt of Nanna in that setting. Suddenly, out of nowhere, a white dove landed at my feet. It brought me to a standstill. It remained at my feet for what felt like the longest time and I remember thinking how unusual the sighting of a white dove is in that part of Sydney.

I knew why the dove was there. The message received was that my Nanna was at peace and she was happy and would always be with me.

My connection to spirit and my realisation that spirit is always with us began that day!

Meditation – It's all about the Cake

by Marilyn McMullen

"The goal of meditation isn't to control your thoughts, it's to stop letting them control you."

~Unknown

What I need is to feel safe, balanced, and connected to the universal energy that flows through and around my body and nurtures my soul. However, I feel anything but …. I am told I have motor neuron disease; here are the test results, what else do you need to know?

The best way I know to find these feelings of safety, balance and connection is through meditation. And, there it is…that wonderful connected feeling flowing through my mind, body and emotions. I feel it deep within me and all around me.

I had been in a similar state before (12 years ago, in fact) when I was told I had an aggressive breast cancer. I remember how I felt that day; I was frightened! I decided I wanted to live, so I placed my physical body in the hands of an excellent medical team and, with the guidance of my energetic healer, I set about healing from within and in time was raised to a greater sense of awareness.

My oncologist was impressed by my progress and said, "I don't know what you're doing, but keep doing it". When I said I was doing meditation she was pleased and supportive, for which I am eternally grateful. Meditation is my mainstay, so much so that friends and their friends wanted what I had (not breast cancer but the calm acceptance that I evidently 'exuded').

So began my life purpose. After the successful completion of my treatment, I studied holistic counselling. In my practice I used meditation as the main tool to assist clients find their truth in healing. I also began practicing meditation with friends and their friends in my home each week. The group of women came for meditation and afterwards we had cake and a cuppa. They developed the skills of meditation and found a sense of calm and balance in their lives. This added to the tools they already had for dealing with their life experiences. One of the women admitted that she originally came for the cake but found that she was sleeping more soundly than she had in years and she was loving how she now felt.

So here I am, not knowing where this diagnosis of motor neuron disease will take me because, unlike breast cancer, there is no medical treatment. I know I am not on my own! I have the love of my family and friends; I have my connection to my own soul; I have trust in the universal energy knowing we are all connected to this energy.

What I do know in my soul is that I can assist my quality of life and my healing through meditation.

Allowing Adversity to Create Good Change

by Jane Woods

"Create the change you want to see in the world."

- Ghandi

I was a mum with three children under the age of four at the time. I cared immensely about the world that I was bringing my children up in. Things were good for us. My husband was travelling at the time and he called me very late one night and told me about events unfolding in America, and possibly in a coordinated way in other parts of the world as well. No one knew what might happen next.

The date was 11th September, 2001. I think we all know what happened. Shock. Horror. Torment. Terror. Such a lot of distress, heartache, loss and trauma. Such a lot of suffering. I watched it unfold through the night. It was unbelievable. How could this be happening in OUR WORLD? The impact of such an atrocity was felt far and wide.

At the time I struggled with the fact that I had brought three innocent children into this world. What could I do to change what had happened? I felt powerless against the strong forces out there that had created this abhorrent situation. Yet within me there was a resistance to simply give in and accept this happening in our world. What could I do? I decided that I would create the change that I wanted to see in our world and I would live with consciousness. I came to understand that while I was powerless to create change in the wider world, I was capable of being the change that I wanted to see within my world. I came to understand that we all create ripple effects with our actions. Be the change that you want to see in this world.

Over the years, I have become aware of the power of forgiveness, the power of stillness and the power of being still and observing what comes up for us. Many times, as we sit with uncomfortable thoughts or emotions, we find that they pass. We can rest assured that there will be external challenges, and our challenge then becomes how we react to them.

We are all individuals, and nobody does us better than we do ourselves. We all have our unique gifts and talents and I implore you to discover and put yours to good use in your world. We are inundated by media at this time in history, and there are many platforms that will try to tell you "the best way" or "how you should look". Be aware that these external influences are just that: external. Always check in with yourself and do/be what is right for you. If we are all able to live according to what we know internally to be right for us, I believe there would be more acceptance and tolerance in our world, which would lead to greater peace, love and harmony.

Since that time, I have been on my spiritual journey. My first callings came from the crystals within the earth. Who knew that rocks could talk? Or create heaviness or lightness of being? I have also learned much from nature, particularly flowers and animals. I enjoy creating community, and I hope that one day we may cross paths.

Follow Your Heart
by Coco Elder

*"Be kind to yourself and have
the courage to follow your heart."*

~ Coco Elder

It was during high school that I had to choose my elective subjects. I loved French and Art, but I was fascinated by a subject called Social Science, where we would learn about childbirth and parenting by looking after a real chicken egg for an entire week. This would involve decorating it, carrying it around in a little basket and diarising its daily outings and events. I was delighted by the various stories that emerged from this challenging task, including students colliding with passengers on the bus home, dropping their baby egg and creating a splattered mess. I was in turmoil as I could only elect two subjects. I knew I wanted to continue with French, but all of my friends were taking Social Science. After much deliberation, angst and teacher counselling, I decided to take Art.

This was later beneficial as my mum had geared me into believing that I would be best suited to study Architecture. This was mum's bygone dream and she fueled me throughout my teen years with knowledge about the importance of good design, free flowing space, and light. I learnt some nifty little terms like architraves, skirtings, fascia boards and, as I topped my year in art, it was clear that if I was to have a recognisable 'profession' in this field, then architecture was the one and only choice.

When the Higher School Certificate results came out, I was devastated. I was a mere two marks off the course that I wanted to study – but mum had another plan. With her savvy secretarial skills, she managed to get me into a degree at the university of my choice to study a Bachelor of Landscape Architecture. If I maintained a distinction average in first year, I could simply transfer to architecture. This never happened. Not because I loved the course but quite the opposite. Initially there were some wonderful subjects that fascinated me including graphics and design, geology, field trips, etc. However, by the time the second year came around I loathed and avoided the work in subjects such as engineering and computer studies. I was going home from university and drawing still lifes and interiors with pastels. What made things worse was, I was staying up all night, and once even two nights in a row, to get the work done for assessment deadlines.

I just preferred to do my own drawings. I loved working with the chalkiness of pastels, using colour, creating textures, and observing the beauty of plants, and the fall of light on objects. It was a mature age student friend who stopped me in my miserable tracks one day and asked me a question that changed my life:

What would happen if I were to die in a bus accident on the way home; could I say that I am happy doing what I am doing having lived my life to the fullest joy?

The answer struck me quite clearly. I wanted to study art post-high school, but I thought it was a 'soft option', something I could always do later in life or in addition to a 'real' career. It took courage to face my parents and make the change. Had I not done so, I would not be a practicing artist today, nor a teacher of visual arts. The beauty of initially studying landscape architecture was that it opened my eyes to understanding how sensitive nature is and the components that make up a particular landscape from the geology, micro-climate, orientation of the land and so much more. It helped me see the geometry in Cezanne's paintings and appreciate the textures and micro-worlds of plants. My favourite genre to paint is landscape. Sometimes, life's setbacks later present as a blessing.

Many people can offer opinions and ideas about what suits others best, but ultimately, I learnt the importance of following my own dreams – to follow my heart.

Trust the Connection
by Luca Orlandi

*"You can't connect the dots looking forward;
you can only connect them looking backward.
So you have to trust that the dots will somehow
connect in your future. You have to trust in something —
your gut, destiny, life, karma, whatever."*

~ Steve Jobs

Steve Jobs, the late CEO and founder of Apple, is quoted as saying these wise words that sum up the magic of connection.

When I connect the dots looking back I can see all of the milestones. The defining moments that led me to my career today as a healer, crystal therapist and Aura-Soma practitioner. I can see my purpose as a healer was obvious but, like a flower in bloom, everything has its time.

When I became curious about pursuing a career in energy medicine, I remember feeling like I needed a 'sign'. After all, it was fair to assume that anyone working in the field of metaphysics must have been born with a gift or experienced a lightning bolt moment that changed everything. How would uncovering a healing gift arrive for a 'reasonable' person like me? Ironically, as a healer, I placed a high value on logic over feeling, so it is no surprise the universe sent me a sign I couldn't ignore – a relationship breakdown and a completely broken heart.

My broken heart became the 'gift' leading me to heal ... along with a little help from my best friend Letizia who suggested I see a crystal therapist. At the time, I was sceptical yet curious; but timing is everything. I had been reading a book by Osho that inspired in me a new way of thinking about ego and the self. As a result, my inner world had started to shift, and so I took a leap of faith and booked in with Laura, a crystal healer.

Much to my relief, Laura was not a witch with a magic cauldron, and she didn't have any chickens on altars. On the contrary, we spent time getting to know each other and had a great chat about Osho. My connection to the universe had led me to the right person, at precisely the right time. Despite this synergy, my logical mind still needed to prove that this healing energy was real.

After some time, I lay on the massage table. At first, I felt nothing, but then something interesting happened. I decided I would visualise energy moving out through the soles of my feet because I wanted a sign this energy work was real. My wish was answered. Within 30 seconds of visualising my feet, I heard Laura's voice. In a calm and meditative voice, she said, "I feel that something is happening around your feet." At that moment, the universe spoke, and my future as a healer came into view.

Connection might start with one moment, one meeting, or one decision that acts as a domino that falls, connecting you to a new path. It might be the link between the future you can't yet see, or the past that only makes sense from the future. It might be something that exists in this very moment. It could be that reading this book, or these words, lead you to the life of your dreams. In the words of Steve Jobs, you have to trust in something, so trust in the connection.

Taking Responsibility for Your Own Life
by Summer Cowie

*"This is the use of memory. For liberation - not less of love
but expanding of love beyond desire, and so liberation
from the future as well as the past."*

~ T.S Eliot

When I was 15 my dad committed suicide. It has been six years since
his passing. This year he would have turned 47. When it first happened,
I remember feeling really lost and confused. I wondered how could a
man, who I thought was so full of love for life, choose to die?

This question haunted me for years.

I have always been open about the details of my life, perhaps because
I never really had the option not to be. I was Mr Cowie's daughter and
his loss drew a lot of attention. When I finished school at 17, I moved
to Newcastle because I was desperate to create an identity completely
separate from what had happened. But my repressed traumas followed
me, and just a year into my new life I wound up in hospital, heartbroken and more alone than I had ever been before.

I now know that I, like all of us, agreed to this life and these experiences before entering into it. I know that I am always supposed to be
exactly where I am. The significance of my dad's loss and the journey
that followed is not lost on me; so the question was no longer 'how

could this have happened?' but 'why this life?' What lesson was I to gain from the childhood and the experiences I had chosen?

The world is brimming with grief. It is our reality, as physical beings, to experience it. Over the last six years my relationship with it has changed significantly because when I remember that my life is temporary and that my goal is growth, even the darkest of circumstances begin to shed light. When I began to recognise that grief and love are just two different ways of expressing the same thing and that all of it is love, something shifted in me.

The impermanent nature of life brings about a variety of emotions and to not feel something that is part of the human experience is a bigger tragedy than death. There is something to be gained from every loss; there is beauty in pain just as there is beauty in every part of life. Losing my dad sent me down a path I never could have imagined; a path that feels like it was always destined. What I once thought of as just a tragedy, something to run from, became an opportunity to grieve so that I could heal. And so, my lesson in grief: in pain is to feel it and to feel it freely. We are human and we are here to feel.

Teacher Aniri

by Irina Gladushchenko

*"Connecting with and guided by the light,
I start my true journey."*

-Irina Gladushchenko

Once upon a time, when time itself was a river, lived Teacher Aniri.

Those in need of a kind word could always come to see him on the peak of the mountain Eceap. He would sit quietly with a gentle, welcoming smile on his lips. In his gaze, the blue vastness of the ocean was found.

The teacher spent his days observing the surroundings, bringing his impression inwards with his every breath. And when they become part of him, he would happily share these heartfelt stories with passers-by and the elements. He felt happy and content as waves of profound gratitude travelled through his whole existence.

But then one day, an unforeseen change in direction shook his world.

One of his visitors shared a sad story about loving parents who were very close to losing their unborn child. This child was a creation of such a unique bond between a man and his wife that it would kill them both if they lost their unborn baby.

Our hero Aniri allowed his very essence to fly over to the foreign land and to unite with the body of a tiny fetus in the mother's womb. Aniri felt very claustrophobic and oppressive but stayed present, and together they made it through the birth.

And what a celebration that was! The whole village was singing and dancing, and everyone was commenting on how unusually wise and peaceful their newborn daughter was! She was just quietly observing her surroundings, trying to make sense of it all.

The only time the baby cried was when her loving mother was trying to feed her. This was just too much to tolerate! She tried to reason with her mother in different ways – using her inner voice at first and, when this failed, vocalising her discomfort by changing the tone of her cries, but her mother was blinded and deafened by her joy. The happiest couple in the world were on a quest to become the best possible parents.

Time flowed as a river does, and our girl turned into a woman and became a mother herself. All her life, she felt that there was another, very different voice inside her, but she was too busy to enquire, floating along the river of everyday life.

Until one day while working on her vision board and looking through magazines, she saw a picture of a beautiful man sitting quietly on the peak of the mountain with a gentle smile on his lips... and they connected.

Ever since that day, our heroine could feel this strong bond between the two of them. And as a token of this bond, she wore a gentle smile on her lips that was identical to her teacher Aniri's.

Energy of Synchronicity

by Corinne Dosoruth and Maxine Pagliasso

encouraged by Irina Gladushchenko and Jenny Fitzgerald

*"Connections can be found everywhere.
But when two paths continue to cross,
it is no coincidence. It is synchronicity!"*
~ Corinne Dosoruth and Maxine Pagliasso

It was week two of the chapter submissions for this book and, within 24 hours, two stories had arrived. A powerful resonance was felt by the project coordinator, and a beautiful warmth and fond memories of her grandmother filled her whole being while reading these chapters about connection and guidance from the other side.

The energy felt too strong to ignore, so the two beautiful authors, and now chapter neighbours, Corinne ('Life Goes on') and Maxine ('She Listens Still'), were invited to explore it further and to co-write a chapter.

Corinne sees her ultimate life purpose is to connect people with hope. She is a very gentle soul, an explorer, a loving mother and wife. Maxine is a strong empath who finds beauty in everything. She loves her family and friends, is mastering the art of self-love and is there for everyone.

Unsure at first, they took on the challenge anyway and embarked on their quest of discovery, connection and co-creation. Starting by exchanging their submissions, these two collaborators were becoming familiar with each others' energies and tuning in to what their chapter was going to focus on.

Corinne shared that, after reading Maxine's story, it was evident that they were destined to meet. "I still feel I knew Maxine from a past life or another dimension. Her story made me anxious, happy, sad, and most of all confirmed that our ancestors are looking after us." They also realised that they met before in person at the wellness centre six months earlier.

The collaborators met up online, but the ideas were not coming together, and the words would not flow. A few weeks later, their paths crossed again as they attended the same online meeting. It was no coincidence that they kept appearing in each other's lives, so they decided to meet up in person at a café.

Maxine reflects, "We talked, laughed, cried and smiled at the cafe. Our feminine energy was heightened, and our stories confirmed that the synchronicity was strong. We left that day knowing that our lives were richer for having met each other."

They discovered how incredibly aligned they were. They are both the firstborn and carried responsibilities that only the eldest child could understand. They are both teachers but of different disciplines. They both studied at the same college two years apart and into their fiftieth year. Both women chose alternative therapies as a gentler, softer career path moving forward into their later life. They also share a strong sense of duty to their immediate families. Above all, Corinne and Maxine feel strongly connected to spirit and divine guidance.

Both agreed that the presence of a more in-depth intelligence was at work. As the conversation continued, the pair marvelled at the synchronicity that was unfolding. The current was so strong that it became possible to articulate it.

Maxine – "I feel synchronicity in my body through my heart space. Synchronicity is an occurrence of a magical moment that should be honoured with love and gratitude. Our heart centre is the space where love and gratitude reside, flowing in and out of us. Corinne and I were energetically receiving each other's love and gratitude that day at the cafe. I might call this friendship therapy that was magically synchronous due to the similarities we both experience in our lives."

Corinne – "I feel synchronicity in my mind, and it flows through my heart and becomes what I like to call 'gut' feeling or a sense of déjà vu! I don't believe in coincidences. I think we are meant to meet some people in our life with the same energy and love of the same things. This is beyond our control and, when we meet, that feeling and thinking that we know that person already is magical."

Maxine – "This journey through life on earth is one of learning lessons and experiencing all of the emotions and senses, whether comfortable or not so comfortable. Now and again, a rainbow bridge appears to make a connection that, under normal circumstances, would not occur. That bridge was built between Corinne and I. It proved to be the most beautiful of synchronistic unions that serve to remind us that there are no coincidences in this life. We are here to love and support one another, to share stories that enable us to learn and grow, and pass those stories onto you, the readers, so that we can all learn from each other."

Corinne – "This journey is magical and proves that some people are meant to meet and enrich each other's life. Maxine and I had similar experiences with our grandmothers, we wrote similar stories and chose similar chapter numbers. Irina also has a powerful story with her grandmother. This is femininity, matriarchy, the moon, powerful energies coming together to create something beautiful. I think our grandmothers are looking at us and laughing right now and even maybe saying, 'We did this.' I hope our stories tell readers that we can connect with our mothers, grandmothers and ancestors, and still feel their love around us and the little or big miracles they send us are no coincidence. It is to help us grow, learn and share."

Finding God on the Cricket Pitch
by Vasu Devi Laura Hamblyn

"God writes the Gospel not in the Bible alone, but also
on trees, and in the flowers and clouds and stars."
~ Martin Luther

I was unhappy. I had hoped marriage and a child would fill the void I felt inside. I had almost resigned myself to living a half-life; coping and making do.

But that was not to be. There was a series of events that would change my life forever. During a very turbulent year (including separating from my husband and some huge heartache), I kept thinking I wanted to run away; to go to India…it just kept popping into my mind.

I would describe myself as an atheist. I was quite anti-religion in my youth, and yet I believed there was a universal energy; an energy that connected us. It was this energy, I believe, that guided me towards meditation. I started meditating and felt such great benefits. Straight away people started smiling at me more. I was able to cope with the day more easily. I was lucky enough to have an amazing friend who taught spirituality. She guided me with helpful books and meditations. This was the beginning! Now, jump forward a couple of years and my friend was taking a group of her students to India and I knew I wanted to go! The logistics were not easy, but everything fell into place.

So, with no real idea what I was doing, I flew to Chennai from London and met up with the group of Australians in the hotel. I was a complete spiritual novice; I recall being on the bus to the ashram and wondering what they were all talking about. Mantras, mudras, etc.; it was a foreign language. I really was running before I could walk.

The trip was life changing! I must confess it was not easy to sit in puja (the act of worship) for several hours as my untrained mind would wander. Invariably, it would get stuck on the 'Is God real?' question or versions of this question. A lot of my unresolved issues were shown to me and were healed, and some good old karma clearing took place. It was quite a rough ride for a few days! I would question, "Well, if there is a God then please show me X", and sure enough X would appear. I did several tests like this; all were answered and yet my mind still questioned.

One day I went for a walk. I wandered out of the ashram complex to a local wasteland where there were several boys playing cricket. It was hot and dusty, and they just had makeshift equipment. As I sat watching them, a sense of deep peace fell over me, as if the light suddenly connected with me. I felt love, I felt God and I felt peace. I remember laughing to myself; all these hours in temple and yet I found God watching cricket!

From that moment on, my ego calmed, I was able to meditate more deeply and there was a lot more joy.

Several weeks after returning from India I recall waking up in the morning and realising I felt happy! This was not a happiness because something good just happened; it was a deep sense of joy. I knew something in me had shifted. The light was shining through, the door was open, and I knew the path my soul was destined to walk. The void had finally been filled.

A Conscious Path

by Norah Copithorne

"Yesterday I was clever so I wanted to change the world.
Today I am wise so I seek to change myself."

~ Rumi

Many years ago, my mind was making all the decisions in my life on its own. My heart had no say and was not consulted. Early on, its irrational behaviour had caused it to be exiled from all strategic planning.

The decision to put my mind in control seemed sensible at the time, but now I'd arrived at a destination full of sharp edges, broken dreams and disappointments. Having invested significant effort to get there, being wrong was unacceptable. And living with the frustration and anger woven through every breath created grave consequences.

One day, I caught sight of my image in a mirror and was shocked at the ugly, angry face that held my gaze. A thin tight mouth with suspicious eyes. Surely that wasn't me? I looked intently at the image grieving the rage emanating from it.

And yes, absolutely no doubt that was me, but so far away from the watermelon grin of my Irish heritage, I might as well have had bad plastic surgery.

What to do?

I had no idea how to move back to a world of kindness, laughter and easy joy. I remembered it and could list the decisions that splintered off into the now but had no breadcrumbs to find my way back. The life I'd created was complicated, restrictive, toxic even – and not my fault! Martyr and victim were common threads in this story.

I wondered and wished to find my laughing self again, completely clueless as to how to begin.

Out of the blue, a woman I'd done some work with decided to pay me $1000 as a consulting fee. Unbeknownst to me, she considered the time we'd spent together having coffee and planning a project that never came to pass as a consultation. She valued my opinion and had to spend money to balance out her taxable income. I was someone she was happy to pay and she said at the time it was the right thing to do. I wondered, totally bemused. Kindness was a foreign concept.

Funded by this windfall, my next question was what next? Where do I find my people? The ones that look deeper, ask questions and explore the intangible passionately?

I invested in a personal development weekend. I met two people that went on to be significant for different reasons in my life, and I went early, had fun, and allowed the pull of curiosity and instant 'like' to guide me. It was a significant start in the right direction.

'Landing' with Love

by Jennifer Nurick

"It was the spirit of my son coming in to meet
me at a time I was fully present, internally quiet
and able to feel him 'land'."

~ Jennifer Nurick

Ever since I can remember, I wanted to be a mother. Perhaps because my own mother had taken on the role so fully, and motherhood had bought her so much joy.

The journey of life took me through the stages of study, travel, work, marriage and immigration. I dove into each of these stages fully, knowing that the time would come to become a mother. My heart always warmed at the thought. In 2007 I could feel the time approaching, so I started to prepare my physical body.

That summer I went to visit a good friend overseas who was due to have her first child. The baby was overdue and finally arrived the day before I was due to leave. Both mother and child were doing well, but there were the usual issues of feeding and soreness after surgery. When I went to visit her in hospital, I was shocked at what I saw. It was all so real, so raw. I suddenly didn't feel so ready to have a child of my own. I remember thinking very clearly, and then announcing to my husband over the phone, something along the lines of, "Oh, no, I am totally NOT ready for that!"

The next month my cycle didn't arrive. I wasn't pregnant. It just stopped. I had been regular my whole life until then. The next month, nothing. The third month, my husband and I decided we would like to start trying to conceive, so I needed my cycle to return. I went to see an acupuncturist and an energetic healer to work holistically on my cycle. I changed my diet completely and started to take supplements. After nine months I went to see a specialist doctor who examined me and said everything was normal and that month, I had what I would call a half cycle.

That same month I went to Cairns to teach an energetic healing seminar. After the workshop I drove up to Cape Tribulation for the weekend on my own. It is a pristine, untouched beach where the rainforest meets the beach. It is one of my favourite places on earth. As I walked along the beach in the sun, I felt my heart suddenly explode with love. It felt like a combination of the warmth of the sun and pure love. I felt a huge yearning for a child, for my child, that I had not connected with before. I burst into tears as I realised how much I wanted this child to come and spoke out loud my love and yearning for him/her.

I forgot about that experience and went back to Sydney as planned. About ten days later I found out I was pregnant! I had been pregnant when I was there. I then remembered that beautiful experience on the beach, the huge expansion in my heart and yearning for my baby to come. I think it was the spirit of my son coming in to meet me at a time I was fully present, internally quiet and able to feel him 'land'. I still feel that same warmth in my heart today when I think about either of my children. Thank you, is all there is to say.

A Story of Hope

by Debra Fidler

*"The only impossible journey
is the one you never begin."*

~Tony Robbins

Everyone has a story, and everyone has a journey. I have learnt to respect journeys, and I now understand that while some are painful awakenings, others are joyous discoveries.

I want to tell you the story of a little girl who loved books. She would wake in the morning to the sound of Clydesdale horses delivering milk in glass bottles. She was happiest jumping off a rope and swimming in the river. Then her sister died and the house became dark. Her father could not bear her laughter and she learnt to be quiet.

She still remembers waiting on the front porch to be picked up by the orphanage with her suitcase. Of course, they never came because her mother decided she could come back in. The memory of not being wanted or loved stayed with her.

When she was 18, she fell in love with a man who was handsome, older, sophisticated, and a little shady. He mixed with the wrong people. She didn't care; she just wanted to be loved. For a short time, it was bliss and she was happy.

A Story of Hope: by Debra Fidler

Suddenly and unexpectedly, she found herself isolated from her parents and in a situation she didn't understand. That was when the violence started. She lived in fear, never knowing when the strikes or blows would start or what triggered them. She learnt to make herself small and invisible. Her lowest point, her ground zero, came when she tried to take her own life. Fortunately for her, and for me, she failed. Because she is me!

That was when my first journey started, my journey back to me. I knew only one thing at that time: I was no longer prepared to hide. It has taken many more journeys for me to have the courage to share. I know that if I can survive my ground zero, then hopefully that can inspire and help others on their journey.

My entire life I have allowed other people's thoughts, expectations, choices and decisions to dictate my life. I created personas to cope. I kept outsourcing the one thing I couldn't give myself – which was love. I couldn't see what this was doing to me and how destructive this was. My journey was remembering and knowing that self-love is about believing, in your core, that you are worthy. That the love you need the most is the love you give yourself. My journey was awakening to love within, being transformed by that love and then igniting the flame of love within.

If the only part of my story that you remember is that I learnt to love myself again, and that self-love created trust and faith within myself so that I could step into who I was always meant to be, then my story will have meaning.

Waiting for Love
by Andrew Head

"I was made and meant to look for you
and wait for you and become yours forever."

~ Robert Browning

Lord Harrgan of Balyan was a kind-hearted soul. One of his deepest life goals was to find someone to love and be loved in return. He didn't want much, he told the lord of all creation, just a companion to share life with and be there for each other no matter what.

One fine day, at a party, Harrgan met and danced with a lovely girl named Belldeen. Belldeen had travelled far for the party, but the two managed to stay in touch and after a couple of months, they realised they had strong feelings for each other and became lovers. At first, everything was wonderful. They enjoyed each other's company and laughed a lot.

But slowly, due to many factors, some Harrgan knew about and others he did not, Belldeen began to change. Gradually, there were some bad times. There were still good times, but the bad times increased and lots of arguments ensued, with Belldeen verbally attacking Harrgan. In the end, Harrgan felt as though he couldn't do anything right and became sad, at times crying himself to sleep. He had tried to love Belldeen as best he could, but she was more and more upset, and not the person she was when they first met. Belldeen would accuse Harrgan of going behind her back with another, and Harrgan tried to say it was all a misunderstanding; he had merely asked a woman for advice on a gift he was buying for Belldeen. Belldeen didn't believe him initially but then eventually accepted his apology.

Time and time again, fights would erupt, Harrgan would apologise, and Belldeen would apologise for being so angry. They would make up, but there was always another fight and Harrgan often had to defend himself about many different issues.

The final confrontation came when, one cold and stormy afternoon, Belldeen accused Harrgan of doing something terrible. All he wanted was to be kind and generous and for Belldeen to be happy. However, her mind was clouded, and try as he might, Harrgan couldn't convince her otherwise. Their relationship over, Harrgan was heartbroken and sought comfort and healing from family and friends.

After a while, Harrgan fell in love again. This time the woman, whose name was Almeera, lived much closer, and the couple were able to spend a lot of time together. Where Belldeen had showed Harrgan what he wanted and didn't want in a relationship, Almeera showed Harrgan just how good a relationship could be. Sure, there were times when the couple fought, but they were always able to talk through their differences calmly, each listening to the other and trying to compromise.

However, Almeera had some family upheaval, and this made her distant for a time. Their relationship progressed into deep intimacy, but there were many times when Harrgan felt neglected to an extent. Almeerra was first on his list of most important people, whereas Harrgan felt that on Almeera's list, her first priority was her immediate family, then her extended family, her friends and number four was Harrgan.

After a long time together, it came to an end because of an unfortunate incident. Harrgan hadn't meant to upset Almeera, but nonetheless she was upset and hurt. She said she needed time to think and after that they would be ok.

Alas, it wasn't to be. Almeera eventually said she wanted to be Harrgan's friend, but not his lover. Because he had experienced a loving relationship with Almeera, he had been so happy and content for most of the time and he tried to talk her round, but Almeera had made up her mind and felt it was for the best.

The second heartbreak hurt so much; it felt as if Harrgan had an arrow in his heart, and a knife in his back. The pain was so great, it lasted for months on end. Harrgan eventually decided he needed to flee. He had family across the sea in the country of Queem, and friends in another country called Zargeth. He had never visited those countries but had always wanted to.

"Now is a good time," Harrgan said to his family. "I am not currently committed to a job, I have savings, so I am going to go visit family and friends and enjoy some time away from my regular routine."

Harrgan had a lovely time away visiting family in Queem, and when he flew to Zargeth, he enjoyed many happy times with friends. One of his friends in particular, Ellie, was a good listener and Harrgan confided in her. Ellie suggested something to Harrgan to help him deal with his loss and give him hope.

She suggested he pray for his future wife. Ellie had prayed for her future husband and found it to be a great experience. So Harrgan prayed to the Creator. He prayed he and his future wife would meet soon, but he mainly prayed for her wellbeing. He prayed she was safe, happy, and all was well for her, wherever she was and whoever she might be.

Harrgan found praying like this was an uplifting and comforting experience. Even though he has looked for years, he hasn't found her yet. He continues looking though, and he still prays for her. He is confident they will meet, and he looks forward to telling her that he had been connected to her through prayer for years and how special those moments were.

Food for the Soul, Body, and Mind
by Sharmini Weerasinghe

"Love of giving is the highest form of blessing."
~ Sharmini Weerasinghe

I learned to cook when I got married in Sri Lanka at the age of 24, to my boyfriend of 10 years. My relationship with cooking started with rice, lentils and canned fish, and evolved into some very delicious meals when we moved into our one-bedroom granny flat. Our home was always open to anyone who popped in at any time of the day. This could have been family, friends, friends of friends, or neighbours, and our way of connecting was to share a meal and spend time with them.

Cooking for me was a way of sharing my love, our home, and to make people happy. For us, sharing gave us a sense of abundance and at no time did we worry we would not be able to do it when starting out as a young couple. My connection to cooking continued even after moving to Australia. It allowed me to share my love for my family, friends, and all those I met. It was my way of showing that I loved to provide food that would nourish their soul, body, and mind, giving them a sense of contentment and well-being.

The only way I can express the way I cook is to say that it is a feeling I have for the herbs, spices, and all the ingredients. When they are in the pot, I can feel the taste, the aroma, the colours of the food without tasting it. It is more like cooking with your spirit or intuition, and I intuitively know what to cook for each person. I feel my love flowing effortlessly through the aroma, creating flavoursome dishes in a very short time. I will know if the dish needs extra salt, spices or herbs, and precisely how much, without overpowering it. I lose touch with time and end up with seven or more dishes, but it is like a blessing to make people happy. I also love it when my husband cooks for me as I can taste his love in the dishes, and it is exceptional.

When guests come to our home, whether they've been invited for a special occasion or they've just popped in for a casual visit, we always offer something to eat. There is magic in the herbs from your garden as they give so much love with their essence, so it is special when you pick your own fresh herbs to cook. Each discovery of a new herb is magical to me, inspiring me to cook dishes with the distinctive essence of that herb to flavour the dish. Each dish is distinctive and never tastes the same, but somehow the recipe stays with me and I am happy to share it with my guest.

My love for cooking is never about eating food just for the sake of consuming something, but rather about sharing the amazing magical essence of ingredients with everyone.

Dance of Life
by Robyn Vincent

"Healing is like dancing – one step at a time."
                                                    – Robyn Vincent

Mary was a quiet, hypersensitive, shy and scared child, doing everything to please others; always doing the right thing. She was ill from six months until the age of two. At two she went into hospital where they tied her to her bed because she wanted to talk to everyone. This was only the beginning of what was to happen in her life.

She had many talents. At three she started classical ballet and tap dancing. At seven she started ballroom and Latin dance. She did drama, elocution, deportment, got roles in television ads and a movie, and participated in eisteddfods for both dance and poetry. Once in high school she gave it all up and played sport – netball, tennis, gymnastics – and learnt piano.

Why did she lack confidence and why was she so afraid?

There was another side to her life. During her early life, she was controlled; though at the time she didn't recognise it as control, she thought it was love and concern. On one hand she was being pushed into the limelight and on the other she was being hidden, which will become obvious shortly.

51

Her childhood seemed normal to her, even though from the outside it was anything but normal. Her father was an alcoholic and her mother was a highly creative, generous, yet insecure woman who helped everyone. Her grandmother and two uncles moved into their home when she was seven, bringing domination, control, abuse (including sexual), fear, as well as more alcoholism.

After leaving school she went on to dance competitively and became a professional. She taught dancing for several years; dance and music were part of her soul. When she was 28 years old, she began working on releasing the issues and challenges of coming from an alcoholic family. She went to many healing practitioners who helped her release and clear these challenges.

Over the years, situations and challenges kept coming back which disturbed her. She realised there must be something else that was not so obvious; something much deeper at the core of her past, requiring her to search more deeply. It was when she was held-up at knife-point that she finally knew she had to get to the core so she could move forward.

One evening it came out that when she was about three, her mother would lock her in a tiny room if she ever did anything 'wrong'. When she first heard this she went into disbelief, shock and total silence – this couldn't be! She'd thought all her pain was related to her father. Later that night the anger surfaced. As she explored the anger, and searched into what was behind the situation, she realised the 'why' – it all fell into place and she'd finally reached the core. It wasn't only being locked up, but the trauma of years of emotional blackmail by her mother and grandmother that had done so much damage. The processes began in earnest of bringing balance back on all levels by going deeper and deeper into her soul.

1998 was a year of processing all the things that had been squashed or controlled in her life. In 1999 she wanted to know more about why this had occurred and felt there must have been karma between them all from a past life. Once she found its origin, she went into meditation to explore it. During the meditation she completely changed that life and the circumstances, which in turn changed the energy in this life. By April 1999 her childhood challenges had finally been integrated.

There would still be other challenges along her path, but the main challenges had been settled.

The challenges that came afterwards made certain that she really knew, understood, believed and accepted what she had accomplished and why she'd had the kind of childhood and life she had. She was FREE!

I See Hearts

by Mel Rourke

"Walk forward with a light heart,
a smile and watch your day magically unfold."

~ Mel Rourke

For as long as I can remember I have had a thing for hearts. My dad and boyfriends would buy me heart-shaped jewellery and I loved drawing them as a teenager. I even got a small heart-shaped tattoo when I was 21 and was inspired to create the Instagram profile @beautyinhearts. For me, back then, they held a surface meaning, representing purity and love. As well as conveying my love and respect for Mother Nature.

I didn't think much of my thing for hearts. I thought it was just where my eye naturally gravitated. I figured, *what girl doesn't like a heart!* Until I experienced adversity, in the form of a loss a few years ago when my heart chakra opened, heart-shaped everything and anything would frequently and randomly appear. Whilst out running, I would see it in heart-shaped leaves, in shadows cast by the sunlight, in the clouds, in rubbish or in gum on the ground. It got strangely ridiculous but felt magical! They had my full attention and I couldn't help but smile each time I'd see one.

During that time, my heart-shaped encounters gave me confirmation that I wasn't alone in my experiences. They were messages or signs which I realised held a deeper meaning; a divine connection and a confirmation of where I was in that moment. They still appear today with messages held for me or those I am supporting. At times it can get overwhelming, as they appear in all forms and sizes.

As I walked at dusk one night, a heart-shaped copper ornament the size of my palm was smack bang in the middle of the path! It was the second largest one I had ever come across. The largest heart ornament is a carved wooden one that hangs from a tree that I happened to be sitting under. This encounter is not so strange, now that I have come to understand that nothing happens by chance!

Late in 2019, I experienced an uncomfortable confrontation, which left me feeling unsettled. As I walked away from the experience to catch the bus, three heart-shaped leaves appeared on my path, one after another. In that moment I instantly let go of what had just happened. I quit analysing it and recognised the experience happened because it was meant to play out that way. The three heart-shaped leaves quickly shifted me out of my head and into a space of gratitude.

Divine messages may appear for you in other shapes or forms. As a star, a feather, a bird, an animal, a butterfly, or as synchronistic numbers.

When you see and recognise divine messages, it's good to check in with what you are experiencing in your current state and consider their significance and what it represents to you, as opposed to googling a meaning. Their significance will eventually become known to you if you want them to. Often their message is beyond what the physical senses allow and it's an inner resonance. With each divine message received, it's also important to show your gratitude, to allow for more to come!

I've come to learn how hearts and the energy of love are hugely significant to where I am on my path today. I see hearts as being a part of my gift and purpose today as an intuitive energy healer and channeler, which is how I share LOVE and connect my clients to a divine love as well as connect them to their own HEART on a deeper level.

The Essence of My Heart

by Lisa Cohen

*"The most common form of despair
is not being who you are."*

~ Søren Kierkegaard

I grew up in a relatively normal household in sunny Sydney, Australia. However, through several experiences as a child and then as a young adult, I came to believe that I couldn't trust my voice, my heart and especially my intuition. What I wanted or believed was not important and my own innate wisdom was not worth sharing.

I let the beliefs, fears and perceptions of others dictate my life path. One day I was given an ultimatum – the man I loved or the job I loved. For the first time in my life I stood in my own power, I stood in my own heart wisdom and chose, what at the time was obvious for me, but a huge surprise for everyone else.

I chose the man I loved!

This one decision to trust my heart, to stand in my own power for the first time ever, has led me down the path of learning and trusting my heart, believing that my innate inner wisdom is worthy of its power and audience.

After having a few children, I decided to study holistic kinesiology to help others connect to their heart and so be able to trust, accept and love their own innate wisdom of love and connection. Within this learning journey I met some incredible mentors and beautiful hearts. I learnt and flourished. I discovered, and continue to discover, what mind-body-spirit connection is and how important it is to my every moment of thriving and intuition.

My thoughts, beliefs and perceptions (many of which were created in my pre-verbal young system), created neural pathways and chemical reactions that became a habit of mind, body and spirit. I became aware of (and continue to discover) the habits of thought, belief and fear that no longer fit or, in fact, were never true! It was the learning to replace these old messages and habits of mind, body and spirit with love, compassion, and gratitude, that transformed my world - my heart essence, intuition, relationships, innate wisdom and connection within myself!

Through guidance in searching for, and discovering my own heart, my past and present can sit in harmony and compassion together. My light and shadow can sit alongside each other. My fear and my love are comfortable in the same space. It is here that my innate wisdom and healing sit in power and abundance. I can hold space and connect with others among their light and shadow, amidst their own searching and mind-body-spirit connection. This is the heart of my holistic kinesiology healing practice.

This path of discovery has led me to strengthen and breathe deeply into the love and wisdom of the 'Divine Feminine'. To sit comfortably and abundantly, 100% ME, in connection to my Creator, my heart essence and innate wisdom - enabling the humble connection to my purpose and light.

Lessons Learnt Along the Way
by James Gillard

"The harder you work, the luckier you get."

~ James Gillard

When I reflect on my journey as the founder of Insurance Made Easy, I feel a great sense of achievement and contentment. Ours is a family business that has grown over the last 28 years into an insurance brokerage specialising in the natural therapies and complementary health market in Australia. Our journey and connection came from my elder brother Glen who, in his late twenties, opened up health food stores and qualified in various natural therapy modalities. Given we are a close family, his journey, in part, became our journey as well.

I went along to several seminars with Glen, and this sparked the opportunity for me to simplify insurance for the natural therapies and complementary health market where there was a lot of confusion about insurance products, services, and complex policy wordings. Just by chance, in 2007 one of our team met up with some key people within the Hypnotherapists Associations and a new insurance product was born, one that now encompasses over 600 modalities.

Mentoring, motivating and assisting employees has always been my key focus. I invest a lot of my time on the workshop floor, working with employees to resolve their queries and problems. I feel the happiest when each person in our team contributes towards a common goal, operating like the different functions of a single organism.

Building trust with our customers is the most crucial aspect of our business and our true quest. To service our clients well requires us to understand their businesses in-depth, so we need to be patient and allow them to get to know us before mapping out suitable insurance programs. That doesn't happen in one meeting. For example, we had ten meetings over six months with one of our clients to refine their insurance proposal before they could present it to their board.

We also focus on delivering great customer service. This comes with various challenges and a need to coordinate a large number of third parties associated in the service delivery. An example of such a challenge is the constant change coming at us from all angles. We have to acknowledge and accept that change is inevitable. The way to keep up in a continually transforming environment is to be educated about the marketplace and the regulatory changes impacting your business and your clients. That way, you can work out how best to respond and help your clients.

There are many things to be grateful for along the journey – however, I would have to say the following two signify my innermost feelings:

- Long term team of staff, who always have the business and our customers best interests at heart; and
- Creating customers for life, many of whom have become close allies and friends.

If I was starting out in business today, I would have secured a long-term mentor who understood me and my business but was not caught up in the day-to-day demands. A long-term mentor provides a sounding board and gives you the confidence to continue. Also, a business partner would have meant the journey would not have been so lonely. When starting a new business, there are very few people you can share your doubts and concerns with. Having a business partner to share the load and drive the direction of the business would have been extremely helpful.

A Turning Point
by Sandra O'Brien

"Better to die on your feet than to live on your knees."
~ Sandra O'Brien

When I left Wellington at 25, after giving birth to my stillborn baby followed by my marriage breakdown, I felt lost and didn't know what to do with my life. But then one day I saw an ad in the paper which was very ambiguous, yet enticing: "Be your own boss, travel, no experience necessary."

I remembered the saying I'd heard so many times from my dad, "A river runs in one direction only, and we have two choices – to follow it or fight against it, but ultimately we'll end up at the same place," and a little voice inside my head dared me to go with the flow. So, I answered the ad. I invited my girlfriend to come along to the interview for protection. I ended up meeting a team of really cool, inspiring young people.

I got the job.

It was, in essence, my own business – door-to-door art selling. I was a shy young woman at the time. I remember how terrified I was whenever knocking on a stranger's door to sell art. But then something clicked, and the whole world became a stage, and I started to play my part. It felt enjoyable, liberating and exciting. For the first time in my life, I felt that I could achieve anything I put my mind to.

We travelled all over New Zealand, selling art, earning good money, building our entrepreneurial skills and making connections for life. One of the most significant relationships was with one particular man on the team, the man of my dreams, with whom I had a daughter.

Later we settled in Auckland as a group. I shared a very luxurious apartment with one of the other girls on the team. We had a bohemian lifestyle, met top musicians, and enjoyed our party life. When I reflect upon that period of my life, I see it as a turning point. It brought me out of my shell, built my confidence for life and showed me my wings.

I am grateful that I could see what I am capable of, that the opportunity presented itself, and that I had the courage to pursue it.

Whale Story

by Jennifer Nurick

"Go under the water with the whales,
they want to teach you about birthing."

-Jennifer Nurick

I was pregnant with my second child, only four-and-a-half weeks to go. It was my mother-in-law's 60th birthday, so we had a big family event planned in Terrigal, about two hours north of Sydney, where I live. On the drive up I started to feel contractions. I put it to the back of my mind; my first baby had come on his due date, so I assumed this one would too. I thought it must be Braxton Hicks, but they were coming every minute or so. When we arrived at the hotel I went to bed and rested, but throughout that evening they got worse and worse.

At about midnight I woke my husband and we went to the nearest hospital. They said I was in labour and because I had tested positive for a natural bacterium, they wanted to induce me. A friend of mine came to help with the labour; she massaged my feet and helped with the process. It started slowly and then the pace quickly changed.

I remember the feelings in my body becoming very intense. I started to tone loudly and asked for an epidural. They started to prepare me for the injection. Internally my mind was somewhere in the Himalayas. I was on top of a snowy mountain toning loudly up to the sky and into the mountains. I remember not wanting to hurt anyone in the room with my energy, so I was 'sending' it to a place that felt safe.

Just then my friend said, "Go under the water with the whales, they want to teach you about birthing." I did as she instructed. I dove into the water in my mind. I toned loudly as I swam with them and their babies under the water and asked for help.

The next thing I remember is feeling the need to push. I said, "Is she coming?" They all looked confused. "I'll check," said the midwife. She checked me and said I had gone from 3cm to 10cm, where she needed to be delivered. There was going to be no time for the epidural. She was coming right away.

I delivered her on the floor with my head on the bed. She screamed loudly as she entered the world and calmed the moment she was put on my body. It was love at first sight. I had gone from stage one to delivery in 40 minutes. The last time it had taken over 15 hours.

That day my family came to visit me. They said, "Oh, you missed something incredible this morning. We saw heaps of whales from the balcony, they had babies! They were playing and breaching, it was incredible, they stayed for ages."

Every year the whales come around my daughter's birthday in October. We always go to the coast to visit them and give thanks for their help in bringing her safely into the world.

Shadow

by Etty Ayalon

"Shadow holds the hidden gift of empowerment."

~ Etty Ayalon

It was the middle of the night, I was alone in my house reading an eerie section of a book on reincarnation when a dark human-shaped shadow appeared in my living room and freaked the living daylight out of me! I jumped off my sofa as it disappeared. I ran to switch on the light and I turned on the television for noise. I was a fearful, nervous wreck and worried the shadow would return.

I spent the next couple of days sleeping with the lights and TV on, thinking this would be a deterrent. I prayed it would not return to communicate with me. My biggest fear was that it might turn up in the seat beside me whilst driving.

I had an inkling of what the shadow was. I was living in Israel at the time and my toxic twin flame was travelling in Australia. He was dark, I was light. We were two extremes of the same soul that split to experience as much as possible on earth. I felt he was the shadow, projecting himself unconsciously into my living room as his thoughts wandered my way. That is how powerful we are!

After a couple of days, I realised I could not continue living in fear. I was exhausted and it was paralysing. I decided to seek help and educate myself; I knew that both light and dark existed and I desperately wanted to stay clear of the dark. Knowledge is power and I was on a quest to regain mine.

I shared my story with my aunt who suggested I talk to her best friend's psychic mother. I picked up the phone and explained what happened and that I was not interested in a reading. I wanted to know what I was seeing. I wanted to know how to work and connect with energy whilst staying clear of dark forces.

I went to visit her within the week. With her teachings I discovered that I could now see energy. She told me I need not fear dark energies and when they appeared, I was to command them firmly to leave and they would do so. She also gave me a long list of books to read by Edgar Cayce, Sanaya Roman, Dr Brian Weiss, and Jane Roberts. I swallowed them up whilst beginning to study alternative therapy for animals, reiki and colour therapy.

Whenever I set up my workspace, I made sure that the light grid was so strong and commanded that no dark forces could enter my space; I did not want anything to do with them. Today in retrospect I understand that the shadow is a gift to acknowledge and work with, not deny. As light bearers, we shine in the dark like a lighthouse, projecting light into the shadows and supporting those in the dark to find their way.

I have come to understand that we cannot do deep inner work without the shadow. It is not to be feared, it is to be respected and honoured when it shows up in our life, to be loved and healed.

That was the beginning of a journey, triggered by my divorce, into asking questions of why this happened to me. As a result, I discovered karma, past lives, parallel universes and so much more. I am learning every day as portals continue to open.

The Song of Healing

by Nina Maudslay

*"The wisdom of all our aspects is within us always, when
we can accept both our darkness and our light we can be
whole. Within the wound lies a great gift, can you see it?"*

~Nina Maudslay

Once upon a time there was a beautiful young maiden named Eden
who lived a joyous and happy life in the village of Wyndara. Her family
cottage was simple and located within a glorious and most abundant
garden. Every day, the beautiful young Eden would spend many hours
in the garden singing and playing, talking to the plants and fairies as if
they were her dearest friends.

She would help her mother who had a bad leg that troubled her
with pain and discomfort. Eden took on house duties – hanging
washing and preparing meals for her father and sister. She had always
helped her mother and often rubbed her leg with a magic balm she
sourced from the wretched old Gangiri woman who lived beyond the
lake, far away on the dark side of the village. Many feared the old
woman, calling her a witch and telling tales of her collecting bones and
feathers for her cave. Eden was not afraid. She loved her mother dearly
and would risk the long, cold trek to Gangiri's cave for the medicine
balm each dark moon when it needed replenishing.

Eden's father Zen was a clever man with many ideas. He would spend hours and days building and creating new gadgets and tools for the builders and miners in the village. Sometimes he would travel to far-off villages to sell his creations and he became well known on the travelling roads. Over time Zen travelled more and more often. He purchased materials and built his creations selling his wares more widely and to many more buyers.

One day on his travels, Zen met a beggar. The beggar was ragged but enticing; he intrigued Zen, luring him in for a chat about a new contraption he had heard of on the roads that could fix a bad leg – giving freedom and movement back – meaning the wearer could walk and dance without pain. Zen immediately thought of his wife Aida and how happy they could be with this new contraption. He daydreamed about how they could dance again as they once had in the days when they were young and full of love.

Zen asked the beggar where and how he might purchase this magical thing. So cunning and clever was the beggar, seeing Zen's heart alight for his memories with Aida, that he convinced Zen to give him everything he owned – his cottage in Wyndara, the beautiful garden and his successful trade business.

When Zen returned home with his news Aida was heartbroken and devastated. She loved their beautiful cottage and garden dearly and how would they live without the income from Zen's trade? And this great sacrifice was for what? Zen had been promised delivery of his special purchase for Aida's leg but it never arrived. Aida raged with anger, and the sadness of what he had done broke Zen's heart too. He felt such guilt and shame that he retreated to the mountains in solitude and sadness.

Aida found a house in a nearby village where she could stay. She had imagined her daughters would join her, but Eden and her sister Freya would not leave their beloved cottage and garden. The next morning a great flood came surging down from the mountains and washed away the village of Wyndara. The cottage and garden were gone. Eden and Freya latched onto the cottage table as they were washed down the river. It was a terrifying ride. The two sisters were cold and alone, waters gushing around them, rough and relentless. They held tight to each other's hands for support and safety and told each other to be strong and brave.

When the fury of the water had died down, Eden and Freya found themselves tattered and torn, cold and alone, washed up on a riverbank in an unknown place. It was getting dark and so they collected leaves and branches to keep them warm for the night. Although she was fearful, and worn with sadness, Eden could not rest. She felt called to the river waters and the moonlight. She carried herself over to the water's edge and bent down to wash her hands in the water. Eden breathed deeply, inviting in the peace and stillness of the night. She felt so much sadness in her being, it hung heavy on her bones and, as she sat with her feet in the water, she caught a flicker of movement in the dark of the river. She wanted to dive deep and search out this life swimming in the dark but instead she stood up and stepped further into the water. She began to sing. Eden sang her heart's song to the moon and stars, to the wise old trees on the riverbank and to the dark waters of the river. Eden's sadness poured out in her song and flowed into the seemingly endless night like petals floating in the breeze. She closed her eyes and sang tears for her mother and father, she sang tears for herself, and she sang tears for lifetimes of sadness before her.

After some time of being lost in her waters and song, Eden felt a soft warmth and glow on her face; the sun was rising, it was a new day! When Eden looked around her she saw that while she had been singing, the bushland animals had gathered to her feet. Ant and fox, deer, wombat, bilby, kookaburra, swallow, kangaroo, frog, butterfly, beetle and bee, platypus and lizard too. They were all beckoning her to come down the riverbank. Eden followed with wonder and curiosity. The animals led her to a cave that looked familiar… Platypus led her inside to where she met Gangiri. She wasn't afraid this time.

Gangiri was unwell; she was cold and frail. Eden lit a fire and sat with the old woman and waited. Over time Eden met with platypus again and again, revisiting Gangiri. She brought wood for the fire and made healing broth, she sang to the woman and with each visit, her strength and wellness seemed to grow. One time, Eden came to the cave, and Gangiri gifted her some beautiful and very powerful wings. They were the most exquisite, soft, mottled white-golden wings Eden had ever seen. "These are yours," Gangiri said, "you must take good care of them." Eden graciously accepted her magnificent gift from the wise, old woman. Gangiri held Eden's hand in hers and said, "Be patient dear girl, as you learn to fly."

Eden continued to visit Gangiri regularly; she felt peaceful there and Gangiri shared more and more of her wisdoms, medicine and healing on each visit. Eden's strength and love grew with her visits and so did her wings. She felt a great sense of freedom with the wide expanse of her wings so soft and strong, and she journeyed often to the salty, refreshing oceans of clarity. She practiced listening deeply and danced often so she could feel into all aspects of her being: the visible and unseen. She became dear friends with platypus, navigating the winters with him and learning his sensory movement. Eden planted a new garden that she tended to and protected daily; she visited this place to find stillness, listen to the hum of the earth and to grow her precious blooms. Over time Eden became more intentional and more discerning with her daily practices that her garden and song became a balm to her and many, many others.

Passageways
by Joan Lewis

"Pain is usually a sign that something needs to change."
-Joan Lewis

It is in giving birth that we as women experience pain, so too is the pearl born by the irritation of sand. The diver in his quest for the magnificent treasure descends to the deep and murky waters, just as the mountaineer treks alone to climb the mountain that is there.

I have found a mix of conflicting 'truths' on my journey to connect. To do no harm and gracefully fulfill a call that asks me to travel and study and expand my consciousness has been my path. I have not realised my greatest dreams or achieved victory in my accomplishments, but have accepted the inevitability of a divine guidance and nature's flow that steers me to my highest good.

Only recently, by the seeds planted in my soul, have I experienced a rebirth. A spiritual rebirth acknowledging Jesus Christ as the one true connection to my God. Jesus said, "I am the truth, the way, and the life; no one comes to the Father but through Me." (John 14:6) In days past I would wrinkle my nose at such a conclusive statement, especially when there are many voices and many paths to God. The maverick in me glides on waves of the quantum field exploring thought-focused reality in a sea of potential… anything can happen if I will it or dream it or intend it…or so I thought.

Then someone said, "It's time to worship the Creator and not the creations." Hmmmm, had I been falsely idolising all that this world has to offer? I love the trees, the sea, the breath of Gaia and the sweetest interactions of wildlife. I love the healing power of heart entanglement and the joy of universal connection….But was I giving it too much attention and not attending to a true connection with the trinity of source…God the father, the son and the Holy Spirit?

Is it in these times, in 2020, that we see the stage of our collective reality and denounce it? Is it in these times that we raise our hands up and really give it to God and accept that we need true loving parenting and direction from a source that holds our best interests? It is just in these times and in these moments that by giving my trust and faith to the Holy Spirit I have been asked to write this passageway to inspire and nourish and give thought.

I've studied ancient civilisations and the timeless wisdoms of Buddhism, Hinduism, the Essenes, native and indigenous wisdoms, and the mystery school of Solomon's Temple. I've practiced the arts of meditation, energy healing, sound therapy and complex activations of our own auric field. I am thinking now that they have all been pathways of wo/man to understand Self. Not that they are bad or unworthy… but they have not led me to this state of grace. Join me in this early transition to attend a bible study or attend a church that teaches the word of Jesus and the joy of the gospels. God Bless.

Born to See
by Lily C Dodd

"Live your life as a dance with the Divine."
~ Lily C Dodd

My name is Lily, and this is my story.

I was born in the far north of Queensland, Australia. I grew up in an Italian immigrant family and my nona had a significant influence on me. She was a woman of prayer and deep faith. I remember her deep love for the Madonna, 'the blessed Virgin Mary', and her vision the night my papa passed. It was a story my cousin and I would ask her to repeat over and over throughout her life. It was the way she told the story that, even till this day, I remember word for word.

I think it was her broken English, her reverence for things that were of a profoundly spiritual nature, and the joy that would light up her eyes whenever she shared this encounter – an encounter, I might add, that she felt so unworthy of having received. Her story was fully integrated into who she was. Her convictions of the ever-presence of the Divine and that the holy angels lived. There was no questioning her on this. I know that it was her love and prayer that has supported me on my own quest into the unseen world.

As a child, I loved roaming with my Aboriginal friends and would often go to school in the morning only to play truant after midday. I would cross the creek, walking through the bush to play and share in the freedom that they had. My love of their stories around a fire, eating freshly caught fish, and learning the deep appreciation of their ways is still with me today. I had my nona's garden full of fresh produce, my friends on the banks of the river, and when I was in these two environments, I felt at peace. On the other hand, my early days at school were the opposite. They were spent conjuring up my daily escape.

I took for granted that I had a natural intuitive gift and one, might I add, that got me into trouble with the nuns! I could see, sense and know their moods. I stood up to them and the injustices that they delivered to us on a daily basis. I think my willful nature of running wild and being free in spirit could not be tamed. I now know that this free spirit is still with me today and my senses still love the feel of the earth under my bare feet, the call of the kookaburra, and the smell of the ground after the rain. You see, I thought that we could all sense the Divine and the unseen world. It was not until my early primary school days that I was told in no uncertain terms, that seeing was for the saints and mystics, not for an ordinary child, especially one with my background.

I'm happy to say that today I love my faith, and I know that my saving grace as a child was that I knew intuitively that injustice was just that: injustice! However, I needed to start my own healing. Out of my own healing came the work that has taken me on a path that I never could have possibly imagined.

My gift was finally accepted and sanctified in the church in a beautiful charismatic mass. This gift has been in use now for over 35 years. It has led me around the world to many people, of many different faiths. Through this, the most beautiful of all lessons I have learnt is that God is love. I have had the privilege to witness many beautiful and miraculous healings and to watch as God has given 'beauty for ashes' – the essence of the Divine nature coming to life in the many I have worked with.

I am pleased to say many of these beautiful people are still in my life today. I now publish a magazine, and my tag line is: 'ordinary people living extraordinary lives'. My life has been a story of restoration, and when we let go and let God in, we can become that which we were called to be. My final word is to keep short accounts, forgive oneself and others daily, and unto thine own self be true.

Wait for the Miracle

by Anastasia Giovanoglou

"Don't give up before the miracle happens."

\- Fannie Flagg

'Be of service' – this has been my inner mantra from as far back as I could remember, probably from the age of five. I felt a strong inner calling from that young age that I was here to 'Be of Service' – and it has been my quest as an adult. My daily morning prayer is, "God, how can I be of service for you today?"

That inner knowing was buried within me for many years, as I tried to survive an abusive and traumatic childhood, experiencing trauma and enduring many painful memories until my late teens, experiencing many episodes of depression and, at times, not wanting to be 'here'.

Then, in my early twenties, I had an epiphany that my challenges were initiations for my spiritual evolution. I realised that my depression was, in fact, the beginning of my awakening; it was a catalyst that propelled me into the life I am living today, as an energy healer, being of service to God and to humanity.

Today, my depression is my emotional barometer, my emotional guidance system if you like, that guides me and keeps me on my spiritual path. I believe that it is through our most challenging and dark times that we have the biggest evolution of our spirit, and that once we can get through those darkest moments, what life has to offer are the most beautiful, magical experiences.

As Fannie Flagg says, "Don't give up before the miracle happens" – and I definitely believe in miracles. Our unfolding journeys can be difficult; healing the parts of ourselves that have been wounded can be a lifelong journey for some of us. It is the journey to becoming whole again that has so many adventures, so I say this quote often and look for the miracles in my everyday life.

When I look back and reflect on my experiences, I am so grateful for them all, for the lessons I have learnt and for the people I have met along the way and to get to a place in my life where I truly love who I am. I often send my challenges gratitude and pink loving light.

As an energy healer using crystal singing bowls, I am starting to really understand energy, vibration and frequency at a deeper level, and how we have the innate ability to heal ourselves — and one way is through sound and vibration.

We all have unfolding journeys and we all have a story to tell. It is through our connection with each other that makes our journey wonderful. It is through sharing and story telling that we can pass our wisdom on to others, to help them and let them know that they are not alone.

May you look for miracles in your everyday life too.

The Breath

by Deborah Shepherd

"Breath is spirit. The act of breathing is living."

~Unknown

Breathing. In and out, in and out. From beginning to end. First and last sound.

A baby's first cry comes with their first breath. We all entered this world with our breath, and from that day onwards, we live with a finite number of breaths. How we use them accumulates into a lifetime of memories. Each breath is as important as the next, and yet we can spend a whole day forgetting to acknowledge they exist.

The breath. It can quieten the mind, allow the heart to open and bring you into the present. The quietness and slow rhythm of the breath can be a guide when things need to reset, giving us time to reflect, to enjoy and savour.

Breathing, a common act for all living, sentient beings. Be it consciously or unconsciously we all do this to survive. Not for one day have we not been connected to our breath. Oxygenating the body by filling the lungs with a universal source of being. Invigorating, revitalising and life-enhancing.

The breath is our master, and servant.

When we are filled with grief, it is our lungs that will enable us to find a way to let go. When we are excited, we bring more in and become fully aware of the breath – be it running, jumping or dancing – we become partners to the rhythm of the breath.

Frightened, the breath can stand still, ever so quietly, not willing to expose us, to alert or bring us out of our place of safety. When faced with despair, it can be the hand we hold that can lead us back to gratitude.

Our planet is abundant with many ways to support us, including the way it recycles our waste and replenishes our breath.

A source of wellbeing, connection and humanity. No matter what skin colour, gender, language, political or socio-economic standing, we all share a commonality of breathing. We often focus on the differences, but when we come back to the breath, we are one.

A healer, a consoler, a nurturer and life-giver.

Breath, our oldest and dearest friend. No matter what is happening in our lives, her constant rhythmic flow lets us know we are never alone.

And when our final hour comes, she leaves with a whisper. One's final breath....

How I became 'Great Moon Heart'

by Elese Barrymore

"When asked who my favourite spiritual
guru is I answered, 'the land'."

~ Elese Barrymore

As a second generation Aboriginal, being in nature is where I feel most comfortable. Although this is part of my everyday lifestyle, I also honour it by treating myself to an annual retreat, usually a yoga and meditation-themed immersion with plenty of solo time and nutritious food.

Open to new experiences, I was called to sign up for a vision quest—a 10-day guided immersion into the desert including a three-day solo adventure into the north, south, east or west. I had heard about the shamanic American Indian teachings of the medicine wheel and felt drawn to deepen my connection to the land and experience these teachings.

As with all pilgrimages, the moment you make your choice, the quest begins.

I was so excited about this wondrous 'sleeping under the stars' experience I had visualised, that I ignored the instructions to pack a tarp and packed an umbrella instead (in case it rained). Little did I know that being in the desert is far from camping in the outback.

Luckily, the facilitator had spare equipment (tents were not allowed) and I quickly realised that my preparation ignorance was, in fact, fear that this retreat was not going to be my usual comfortable retreat experience.

As I integrated with the land and my surroundings, I sat with the fear and felt my true size stripping away all of society's comforts and distractions. As I shifted this awareness to a level of acceptance, I regained my confidence about the three-day solo segment that was quickly approaching.

Armed with a tarp, clothes, minimal toiletries and nine litres of water, I set out into the west, confident that the next 72 hours were going to provide some kind of enlightenment, as was my original intention.

When I returned to basecamp three days later, I did have an enlightenment experience to share, though I never imagined it would come through such a struggle. I could hear the wind coming from kilometres away and with it came many voices and messages. The darkness, even with a full moon, made me confront shades of my shadow side that I did not know existed. And three days without food has its own layer of physical and mental challenges.

The enlightened result: I survived. I survived harsh conditions and grew to respect and honour what started out as intense fear. I learnt through personal experience that I can, in fact, survive anything. I learnt the real value of connecting with mother earth and being guided by father sky. And most importantly, that the land will always provide. In the depths of fear, the smallest gesture such as a visit from a native animal can bring joy. The trees provide shelter and much-needed shade. And water really is our single most important resource.

With this knowledge and experience, I returned to normal life with a deeper sense of gratitude for the environment I call home. Planet earth in this universe. As I turn inward, I fully realise my being is exactly the same — an eco-system that exists within a larger eco-system. All made up of stardust and consciousness, ultimately connected by love.

You do not need to travel to the desert to experience this connection.

It is your bare feet on the ground, the sun on your skin, and the syncing of your breath with the trees.

Van Gogh

by Amy Morse

"There is safety in the midst of danger. What would life be if we had no courage to attempt anything?"

~ Vincent van Gogh

During my travel to Valencia, Spain, I was lucky to see the 'Van Gogh' live experience. It was a journey of discovery into this amazing artist's fascinating life. The event captured the phases of Van Gogh's artwork and life as they shaped and evolved over time. It displayed floor to ceiling screens as dramatic music played, with quotes and information of his sad and tragic life.

Van Gogh was a troubled, eccentric man who suffered with mental illness. It is believed that he took his own life and died aged 39 (1853-1890). A brilliant artist and a loving, sensitive soul. His emotions were expressed in his art, beautiful words, and quotes. Unfortunately, he lived in poverty throughout his life, and his talent was highly unrecognised.

He was generous and profoundly kind. He inspired great loyalty. He had a close relationship with his brother Theo who was his main source of financial support throughout his life. His parents regarded him as a 'social misfit' and sent him to a mental asylum.

He had trouble with love and had two unhappy romances, which were not sustainable and resulted in unrequited love. He was infamous for his act of cutting off his ear, and giving it to a prostitute called Rachel, during a psychotic episode. However, literature suggests that Van Gogh did this as an empathetic gesture. He was deeply misunderstood.

'The Red Vines' is the only painting he sold while he was alive. It was sold in Brussels for 400 francs. He had five years of false starts and rejections and did not know what to do with his life. He originally thought his calling was to be a preacher, but it took him years to discover it was art.

Today, Van Gogh's paintings are among the world's most valuable paintings: for example, 'Starry Night' sold for $82.5 million in 1990. The Van Gogh Museum in Amsterdam holds the world's most expansive collection of his work.

Van Gogh said, "I feel like a failure". It is hard to image that someone with such talent could feel that way. Sadly, his life was over-shadowed by mental illness. Van Gogh began painting when he was 28 years old and died 10 years later. Imagine what he could have done had he lived a longer life.

Insight into his life provides a powerful message for us to continue to pursue our dreams in life. Not to be disheartened by failures and when things do not work out. We never know when something amazing is around the corner. It is important to have the courage to attempt what we think is impossible, and never give up.

His soft and emphatic personality is an example of kindness; the kindness and love that we need to show ourselves and each other. Van Gogh was considered odd; however, if you think something is strange, perhaps you need to look a little closer.

"I feel there is nothing more truly artistic than to love people." - Van Gogh.

Connection Within: Refuge in the Body

by Elle Reynolds

"Your true home is in the here and the now."

~Thich Nhat Hanh

Of the many connection experiences I've had in my life, I want to share a recent one. A story of deep connection and peace, in the face of adverse circumstances.

My recent birthday prompted me to set some intentions for the coming year as well as the next decade of my life. I went within and found guidance that called for me to stop adventuring, questing and building; and to settle into peace, calm, warmth, community and presence. On my birthday, in the presence of a circle of dear friends, I welcomed the guidance in and set the intention. May it be so!

Within a few weeks the coronavirus pandemic hit, and the world around me descended into the exact opposite of my intention – fear, panic, lockdown and hardship.

In my life I had leaned into enough waves of fear to know that on the other side of fear is blissful liberation. So I anticipated with curiosity what was on the other side of this fear, and worked to lean into these collective waves, often not knowing whether the fear was mine or if I was feeling it from my community, locally, nationally or globally. The leaning-in drew me back to my body, back to the immediacy of the present moment, back to how this beautiful vessel I lived in was feeling, right now.

And I sat with it and was curious – what is here in this fear; in this constriction; in this feeling that the world is crumbling around me? What exactly am I afraid of right now? Is it the collective panic, is it being controlled? Is it pain and mortality? OK, this is me feeling fear; this is how this vibration of fear sits in my body. Can I accept it and get to know this place? A curiously beautiful connection was happening within me, as I got to know myself while fear was swimming around me.

And as I got to know this terrain within myself, I was drawn to return to my physicality and my warm, nurturing surroundings repeatedly. To keep recognising the truth: I am safe in this moment; I am well; I am protected and supported.

I softened further into my yoga practice, finding refuge deeper in my body. This truth was present throughout my body too – I am here in my beautiful tranquil yoga space, I clearly am safe, I am well, I am supported. My body opened and softened, letting me feel the dance with gravity that we do each day, feeling each exquisite movement, each shift of nerves and flesh. In the midst of the fear pandemic, my connection with my beautiful physical vessel was deepening and strengthening, my experience of embodied safety and calm was becoming more tangible.

And how does this reconcile? How am I surrounded by panic and yet able to feel these exquisite times of presence, warmth, safety, reassurance and peace? Maybe I don't need to rationalise it, to chart the course and figure out 'how to'. Maybe the embodied experience in this time is enough in itself, for me to nestle into and draw on in the journey forward.

This beautiful connection within me and with a supportive physical world around me is a gift, to be cherished as a jewel, and expanded as I walk forward in my life. My birthday intention is weaving its magic, taking me through unexpected places as I loop back towards my destination – a deeper connection within me and my world.

Fairies, Readings and
Spirit Guides Whispers
by Kristy Ismay

"Stay in your sparkle. You are divinely surrounded,
supported, guided and loved. Embrace the magic."

~Kristy Ismay

There is so much magic happening in and around our everyday lives. We've come so far on our journeys, and we sometimes forget just how far we've come. We've lost track of how much we've grown, learnt and remembered. We start to take our gifts, abilities and connections for granted. Our sixth sense, our ability to tap into the divine source that is constantly supporting us and guiding us. Tapping into other realms, to guides, angels and yes, even fairies… to intuitively see, hear, feel, and know.

There is so much at play beyond our physical world, and yet the beyond is right here – our connections to this human life, our connections to higher realms, and loved ones who have passed over. There is so much guidance and support at our fingertips… we keep being shown this through numbers, signs, synchronicities and spirit guide whispers.

I was guided to see a psychic medium; first just by thought and then by a physical sign in the form of a chalkboard with her name on it. She was back at the local bookshop I often frequent. The last time I saw her was seven years prior. I asked myself, did I really have the funds for this appointment? I took her business card and looked her up online. Noticing that you could only pay via PayPal led me to log into PayPal which, by the way, I never use. To my surprise when I logged in, I realised I had a credit in my account – enough to pay for the session. I was baffled but went ahead and booked.

Despite being heavily booked, I got an appointment for the following day. It was meant to be, right? But it gets better. As I sat down for my reading, I advised her that I had paid for the half reiki/half psychic reading. She explained that she wasn't really doing the healing side anymore. I shrugged and said, "Well, the full hour reading is meant to be then." We had a wonderful chat about my strong connection to those in the spirit world, on my mother's side. I was also connected to much higher guides that had been with me for many lifetimes but never had a human incarnation. She explained there was a male energy that actively wanted to work with me and help me. I had felt his presence and guidance many times before.

It was the same presence that led me to college to complete a diploma in energetic healing, just a year prior. We continued our conversation and the reading, and I explained how my energy healing sessions worked for me and my ability to hear, see (impressions of clients' loved ones who have passed over), physically feel and intuitively know.

The medium doesn't visually see spirits but is connected through hearing and feeling. It was in that moment that I realised just how much I had been blessed to be able to connect intuitively to my spirit guides. It really highlighted for me how much I had taken these gifts for granted, like they were just part of my everyday life.

As I thanked her for the session, she asked me to bring back my business cards. She asked if I'd be happy for her to refer anyone interested in healing to me. Needless to say, it was a big "Yes" as I pulled a stack of business cards from my bag.

On the way home, I tuned in to this male energy spirit and asked for a sign that he did, in fact, want to connect and work with me. I asked what the sign would be to confirm that I was communicating directly with him. I was told, "You will receive an angel or a fairy". It was as clear as day. A car drove past on the opposite side of the road with the number plate 'KI.222' – KI being my initials and 222 an angel number. I came home and wrote this in my journal, and I never told anyone. I'm also now laughing because receiving that message was my communication with him.

Just a few days later on the 22nd (another 22), imagine my surprise when I went to the letterbox and, in a plastic zip-lock bag, were four miniature fairies: one pink, one aqua, one mauve and one yellow. I was elated to say the least! Blown away. "You will receive an angel or a fairy" – I certainly did. No note, no address, no sender. It was absolute confirmation of our connection in physical form.

This life we are living is full of sparkle and wonder. When you take the time to connect to the divine and your guides, LIFE BECOMES MAGICAL.

You are enough, you know enough, you intuit enough, you are loved and supported and backed in every way.

Bone Woman ~ Shamanic Mystic
by Yia Alias

*"As women start to take responsibility for their own story,
they liberate dismembered soul parts, not only of their
own hereditary patterns, but the inherited cultural belief
systems, and in this space something new is born."*

~ Yia Alias, Womens Mystery eJournal

'Bone Woman' is a powerful archetypal force that I experienced from the depths of this ancient landscape. She burst through my body /mind /emotions, heralding the beginning of my peri-menopausal journey in my 42nd year. Her voice echoed loudly into the core of my being: "Let Go! Let Go!"

My role as a comforting, breast-feeding mother was ending and I experienced great grief weaning my last child. The new me had not yet been dreamed up; my old pre-mothering model no longer inspired. I had to surrender and trust this frightening space of the void. Out of this nadir emerged old traumas, memories of childhood, suffering, abuse, all those things that had been sublimated so I could cope.

They now demanded my attention.

I became ill and almost died from pneumonia. Feelings of shame, marginalisation, insecurity, fear and doubt rose out of this dark space like shadows seeking light. The internalised values and concepts of beauty I held fell away. I was unmasked and utterly stripped down, like my skin had been scraped away to reveal the bone underneath. There was no distraction great enough to hide behind. Like the myth of Innana, where she descends into the underworld and is hung on butcher's hooks and left to rot, I was left bereft.

It became my mission to re-story my Self, to rebuild myself with things that had meaning, that had truth, sacredness, and substance. I did this through ritual and dance, consciously farewelling the old, and calling in the yet-unknown version of myself. A new identity started birthing, and with this birthing came aging. And with aging came eldership and new responsibilities.

It has been over 20 years since 'Bone Woman' called me to wake up. She heralded a new beginning and set the stage for the slow and sometimes painful journey of menopause into early eldership. In my work now as a counsellor/mentor, I witness a version of 'Bone Woman' in most of my clients journeying through the threshold of the 6th septennial, ages 42-49, which aligns for most with the peri-meno-pausal/ autumn season of a woman's life.

This feminine presence expresses as a shamanic mystic and conscious journeyer. She restores herself on her own terms with values that resonate from deep truth and love. She transmutes old stories to bring healing back to community and has the power to transform the wreckage inflicted over eons; of power over and disrespect of women and this planet.

'Bone Woman' is a transformer, a processor of our dormant wounds, a truth speaker and she bares her scars as adornments. 'Bone Woman' has the ability to midwife/ birth/ support new ideas. She is the designer for a future that is unfolding with every breath.

Women are awakening: The groundswell has burst the banks!

She says No! to the sanitising of the human experience. No! to the disrespect of the planet. No! to the filth of pollution. No! to violation. No! to rape. No! to humiliation.

What a blessing it is to be present in these times to witness this shift. The power of the divine feminine will not be held back any longer. She is here!

Living Buddhas
by Elain Younn

"Happiness will never come to those who
fail to appreciate what they already have."

~ Buddha

Once a upon a time there was a woman who lived in Japan. She
worked all day keeping very busy, and when she had any free time, she
would walk through a bamboo grove to visit an ancient temple. It was
a majestic temple surrounded by lush gardens. Before going she would
spend hours making food to give as offerings to the monks who lived
there. She would donate whatever money she could spare. She would
spend hours on the weekend kneeling, in deep prayer, meditating in
front of the most peaceful looking buddha statue. One day while she
was deep in prayer, in a semiconscious state, she saw the statue glowing
and heard it speaking to her:

My dear child, why are you here? Why do you spend all your money
and free time praying to me when your mother is waiting at home to
spend time with you, when your husband and children are hungry for
your affection, when your money can provide some comfort in their
lives. I live inside each and every one of you. Connect to your family
and you will find me. You don't have to come to the temple to do that.
Go, my child, and be with your mother, husband, and children. They

are waiting and longing for your presence. Your presence is all that is needed, nothing more.

Then all was silent. She realised how she had neglected her loved ones and, with grateful tears, she stood up and walked back home. Now her home is her temple and her buddhas are living buddhas.

Coming Home
by Izabella Jokinen

*"It is our light not our darkness that most frightens us.
Our deepest fear is not that we are inadequate. Our
deepest fear is that we are powerful beyond measure."*

~ Marianne Williamson

I was recently contemplating this beautiful topic of connections and,
for an extended period, I became side-tracked or even blocked by the
idea of human connections. My story stalled numerous times, it simply
wouldn't come together until I finally let go and allowed the story to
flow through me.

Throughout my life my deepest regrets always came from forgetting
who I truly was and severing the connection with my divine self. This
unplugging from my own source always brought me the greatest pain;
the most significant life lessons and often the inability to genuinely
connect with others, even those closest to me. After many repetitions
of the same conditioned behaviours, I now realise that the problem
largely stemmed from the fact that I simply doubted my universal
connection and maybe even feared its greatness. I would vehemently
ignore my own internal spark and suppress its loving guidance only to
eventually rush back searching for it in desperation.

The hamster wheel lessons that surfaced in my life always appeared

94

during a period of disconnection. It was then that I would allow my human blinkers to take over, becoming one with the dark, busy, all-knowing wolf once more. The intensity of this ego-driven behaviour would allow the joy to seep out through the cracks of my already patched-up soul. The frustrating heat of repetition melting away the golden glue of light that my spirit had placed there the last time I allowed myself to heal.

It is during these periods that I forget to ask for help, my health suffers, and my relationships begin to gently fray, like the edges of a poorly maintained fabric. My body always shrieks with signs, the all-too familiar aches and pains, the dread within, the discomfort, confusion, inability to move forward; they all act as messages from my soul screaming to me with the hope that I will finally hear its desperate pleas to bring me home. My only job was to dissolve my ego for long enough to listen.

It is well known that our lessons, if left unlearned, will return to haunt us over and over until finally, the duality is somehow banished, and we return to grace, simplicity, and a gratitude for ourselves. It is always then that we are given a brief interlude to choose a renewed relationship with who we are. This provides an opportunity to return to our core of unconditional love; that beam from which we originated, and to operate from there once more.

It is my greatest hope, firstly for me, because like all of you reading this, I too deserve this prayer, that my story is like a mantra on a prayer flag caught by the wind and gently blown out into the universe, where it can touch as many souls as possible, helping to bring us back to ourselves. That all-knowing, all-loving, deepest of connections, where we can always find the greatest instant relief, healing and our soul's true direction.

Modern Blessing of Ancient Wisdom
by Julia Pomazkina

"Ring the bells that still can ring,
forget your perfect offering.
There is a crack in everything -
that's how the light gets in."

~ Leonard Cohen

I am travelling to India! Finally! Finally, I managed to get five weeks leave from work to travel to the country that has called to me for many years. I prepared, I read many fiction and travel books on Indian culture and heritage. I even took a Bhagavat Gita course. When the plane landed in the old Bombay airport of 2006, I remember breathing in the hot airport air and thinking, "I am home".

Excited, curious, at times overwhelmed by a variety of Indian experiences, on my last week of travels I ended up in a yoga ashram in the South of India. The ashram offered four hours of daily yoga, Vedic studies and a cultural program. It is there that I heard the word 'Ayurveda' for the first time. I went to a Vedic medicine lecture, and I still remember the Ayurvedic doctor talking about Ayurvedic consti-tutional types. Vata Pitta Kapha – new words… we are all made up of the same elements, physically and energetically – he was saying – but in different proportions. We are made of the elements of air, space, fire, water and earth – and we need to look after their correct balance in our bodies and our psyches. We are all the same, but we are all unique. He was talking about correct eating, correct exercise, yoga, pranayama and spiritual practices for each Ayurvedic constitution.

Interesting, I thought. So true, so profound, so elegantly weaving together material and subtle aspects of human existence. So challenging to the western way of perceiving and analysing things. The doctor's words carried the wisdom of the many-thousand-years-old tradition.

I visited the ashram Ayurvedic centre after his talk. This is where I had my first Ayurvedic massage – warm earthy fragrant oils poured on the body seemed to melt away many years of underlying stresses and overwork. A few years later, while studying at an Ayurvedic centre in India in 2010, I witnessed the intricate preparation process of Ayurvedic oils and herbal medicines. Truly unique, very laborious, in strict accordance with the ancient scriptures. Large vessels with oil are boiled with specific herbal decoctions for hours and hours, then cooled down – then more herbal decoctions are added to the same oil and the process is repeated. Preparation of Ayurvedic oils takes many days – if not weeks – and makes these oils into very potent healing substances. Watching it, I was thinking of how fleeting and vulnerable yet how strong and precious our human life is. A gift, a tiny gracious moment on the cosmic clock. And that's what Ayurveda remains to me – a gift. A gift from the ancient seers, sages, saints and scholars. A gift from my teachers whose dedication has touched my heart. A gift from my patients who inspire me. A gift, teaching us how to nurture and value our life - 'ayur', from the first breath to the last.

Upon returning to Sydney in 2006, life took many twists and turns. Many other trips to the ancient land of India. Completing an Ayurveda certificate course in Sydney in 2010. Discovering other amazing modalities including energy healing. Burning out in my corporate career. Completing a three-year Advanced Diploma in Ayurvedic Medicine, the highest Ayurvedic qualification in Australia. Opening my Ayurvedic clinic. Studying with many inspirational teachers, to whom I am forever grateful. Learning to live the wisdom of Ayurveda....

Sisters

by Debra Fidler

"We are sisters. We will always be sisters. Our differences
may never go away, but neither, for me, will our song."

~Elizabeth Fishel

As we journey through life, we all face battles and often meet them thinking we are alone. I am not sure why we forget that we are loved and that support, both physical and ethereal, is available. My sister and I were loved unconditionally by our parents who were navigating life and family and doing the best they could for us.

My sister is seven years younger than me and for many years she battled with the belief that she was only conceived to replace another sister who had died. My battles were different, and it really impacted her when I was estranged from the family. In her eyes I was no longer the supporting presence in her life and despite our many arguments, the paradox of sisterhood meant I remained her lifeline and heroine.

I still remember being 12 and getting my first record player for Christmas. I felt so grown up. My sister got a big purple elephant. I don't remember how it happened, but that elephant was thrown at the record player and destroyed my precious 'David Cassidy' record. I was distraught. My dad responded by telling me the story of the *Jungle Book* and the ape who wanted to be like the humans. He told me about the song 'I wanna be like you'. He wanted me to know that my sister thought the world of me and wanted to be like me and that is why she had reacted the way she did.

Another memory I have is being at the local shopping centre and having to sit with my sister watching a pantomime because she refused to be alone. Our mother was shopping, and I was sitting watching Cinderella, with my sister! I have many memories like this and for me my only memory of a sister, is her.

I also remember being so frustrated with my sister that I once gave her five cents and told her to go and buy an ice cream. I went back to reading and off she went. I was responsible for her and I was so frightened when she did not return and couldn't be found. My sister was also in tears, but for a different reason: she had lost the money.

My sister and I have been fashion designers, nightclub owners, holistic entrepreneurs and agents of change and always wanted to have a business together. I do not think we realised that deep in our hearts we simply wanted connection. When our mother died in July 2019, we came to the realisation that it was time to actually start something.

It has taken us 25 years and the death of both parents to rediscover the bond, connection, and depth of our relationship. A bond that was always present, even if I was unable to see it.

We have journeyed separately. We have faced our inner demons, challenges and became individually stronger. We have faced many battles alone that we could have faced together. Today, however, we face life united as sisters. We are a family that has a beautiful and collaborative relationship and we share the laughter, the tears, the frustration, and the anger, together. We are united in the belief that we are both here to serve and we are passionate about enabling change for other women. We honour the tenants of truth, spiritual wisdom, and different ways of knowing and learning.

We are sisters.

Why I Birthed My Business
by Avanti Singh

"We are all portals in which the divine, creative force comes forth and transforms from the spiritual world to the quantum world and finally to the material world through the process of birthing."

-Avanti Singh

The birth of my sister's first baby would forever change me. The arrival of my gorgeous little niece in 2003 shook me to my core, unleashing a deep desire to have a baby of my own. By this time, my husband and I had been together for some time and it had taken me a long time to decide to have children because of a neurological condition and scoliosis that I had battled with for most of my life.

Although I am blessed to be born through beautiful parents, I had a tough time emotionally and physically from childhood contending with these conditions. In 1999 and at the age of 29, I eventually decided to have major spinal fusion surgery with the insertion of thoracic rods and screws along my spine to help stop the curve from getting worse and removal of part of my ribs to reduce the protrusion. The six months of recovery was challenging but it brought me Yoga as a path for living and ignited my passion for learning and integrating health practices into my life.

However, embarking on having a baby was daunting for me because I did not want my child to end up with the same conditions that had dominated my life. After genetic testing and doing some research we decided to undergo pre-genetic diagnosis through IVF in order to have a baby.

This journey began in 2007 and quickly into this process I realised it was clinical and streamlined; blood tests, ultrasounds, needles, packs of stuff! When the first round 'failed', the doctor advised us to not think about it too much and just do the next round.

We did not listen and took a break. The first round felt like a shock. It was difficult for me to accept that I was not pregnant, particularly because of all the preparation I had done since 2003. Every thought I had was on pregnancy. I became obsessive and was totally unaware of just how much my limiting beliefs and fears were taking over. The hormones had really started to affect me as well, but I just got on with it. I did the physical part very well; I ate wholefoods, exercised regularly, my husband injected me routinely with IVF medication, everything was regimented, ordered and precise.

Looking back, I realise how disconnected I was from myself and everyone around me including my husband. I did not seek support from my friends and was even guarded with my close family members who tried to help as much as possible. As a couple though, we did have one counselling session at the IVF clinic but did not feel happy with the way it went.

We tried another round at the end of 2007 and this time I got my period before the first blood test, which devastated us. In April 2008 we were about to have a transfer of our last frozen embryo, but it did not make it through the defrosting process.

By this time, I was so numb that I did not even react to this. I was so lost by now that I could not even connect to the disappointment, the sadness, the inexplicable emotions. I broke down and walked out on my marriage and my life as I knew it unravelled.

This great chapter that started with the arrival of my gorgeous niece in 2003 shifted course with the birth of my beautiful nephew in 2009.

It was at this point that I truly started to drop deeply and fully into all the 'yuck' emotions like shame, fear, sadness, guilt, anger...., probably for the first time ever. Dorothy was finally awake on her walk down the yellow brick road.

Today, I am aware of so many factors that led to my life breakdown. It was the awakening I needed, to be honest. I learnt to open up to all that is within me and this led to such a beautiful and deep connection to the sacred, to the divine, to the mystical, to the unfolding of my truth, to my co-creator, to the unlocking of my potential and to my perfectly imperfect and purposeful life.

Everyone's journey through IVF is different and everyone's journey through having a baby or not having a baby is different. To me the 'baby making journey' is not necessarily only about having a biological baby. It is about creativity, spirituality, the mature feminine, Shakti and Shiva and so much more. It can be transformative and powerful and an opportunity for re-writing one's story, returning to our heart, to spirit, to wholeness and to living the life we are meant to, if we allow the divine to work with us and through us.

I birthed my holistic counselling and meditation business called 'My Prana Portal', meeting place of ancient wisdom and modern science at 11am on the 11th of the 11th, 2011. I call it 'my great birthing experience and labour of love' and it is my way of uniquely and divinely contributing to this beautiful universe.

What I recognise, and what we all have the opportunity to recognise is that whatever we birth 'comes through us and not to us', to paraphrase a famous saying. We are all portals in which the divine, creative force comes forth and transforms from the spiritual world to the quantum world and finally to the material world through the process of birthing, if we allow it ;).

A Question or Two
by Jane Woods

"There's an unseen world out there;
we just need to tap into it."

~ Jane Woods

For about six months I had been on my 'spiritual journey'. Things were 'same, same, but different'. I was aware that I was looking for my own answers to questions that weren't the norm. When I tuned into my guidance, I was guided to attend a crystal healing course. Within this course, they talked about auras and chakras, of which I had no knowledge at the time. We did various exercises with the crystals; some of these were individual, others were in pairs; and we also did group exercises. We meditated with the crystals and placed them on our chakra points.

Although nearly 20 years have passed since that time, I still recall some of the crystals that I worked with and the messages that were transmitted to me by paying attention to them. I became an avid collector of crystals and at home, I dug out the few crystals that I had collected over the years and through experimentation, learnt how to tune in to their energy again.

While I continued to explore the world of crystals, I also started attending a meditation class. Our teacher was very structured and told us that we needed to meditate twice a day for 20 minutes. I found this very challenging, so I was pleased that I was able to succeed despite lots of distractions. The type of meditation was one using a mantra. We were given a mantra, and we were given a choice to use this or come up with one of our own. Our teacher believed that we should use the same mantra for years. I stuck with it for the term, and something clearly shifted within my vision and heightened the awareness I had of my senses.

I remember one morning, I woke up early and went downstairs to lay on the couch. I looked up and, to my amazement, there was an emerald green cloud that moved towards me and sat next to me on the couch! What was most amazing to me was that I could see this with my eyes open. As I watched the cloud, I became aware of something else in my peripheral vision emerging from the same spot as the cloud. This was a paler form; it had a translucent, ghostly appearance of a man. Most notable was a hole through his body. I sensed that he had been shot.

I became scared, not only by what I was seeing but also because the energy I felt was very heavy and sad. I did not scream as I might have done a few months prior. I followed my intuition and calmly said, "Only good surround me now," and watched as this apparition faded away. The green cloud remained a little longer, and then it disappeared as well. My questions increased, and I remain hopeful to find answers.

Signposts for Life

by Sheila Fawns

"Always trust your gut instinct."

~ Sheila Fawns

When I was nine years old, I had a penfriend, Elizabeth, who lived in Australia. I was living in bonnie Scotland at the time. We would write to each other once a month or so, way before the age of emails. Elizabeth was a distant relative of my grandmother who was keen for us to keep in touch and so we did. Elizabeth was a couple of years older than me but we seemed to have a lot in common. One day I received a gift from her. She had sent me a set of nine postcards all joined together of different places in Australia. I had never seen anything like it and it was so special to have this from the other side of the world; it quickly became very precious to me. When I first glanced through the nine postcards, one of them was of a very special fountain in Canberra that looked like a snowflake. I immediately had the thought, 'This was where I need to go'.

Years later when I met my husband, we were discussing getting engaged and I said to him, "Well that's all very nice but I am going to live in Australia." His reply was, "Well, ok then." We left Scotland to live in Australia about three years after our engagement. That was almost 38 years ago - we are still here with three Australian-born children! The power and certainty of my nine-year-old self still astounds me. Almost all of my family have followed me to live here: my mum, my dad, my sister, one of my brothers, a cousin. All because when I was nine years old, I trusted my instinct, my inner knowing, my intuition! Signposts for life!

Finding 'The Mother'

by Carmel Glenane

*"Allow your heart to receive through
the one of every living thing."*
~ Carmel Glenane

My quest to find 'The Mother'; 'The Divine Feminine' created itself through 'The High Priestess'.

Where, how and why did this happen to me?

The tragedy of my husband taking his own life left me financially, emotionally, and spiritually bankrupt. I felt loss and abandonment to my core. I decided my quest to recover was in finding the path of the heart, through salvaging myself, my family, and my business. Trusting in a 'force' to support me became my only desire. I struggled with core identity issues and was ready to abandon my business which I had established in spirituality, healing and teaching.

I needed answers and I needed them fast. The true catastrophe of my financial situation became evident as I realised I had no home, car or money through his embezzlement.

"Draw on your own magnetism and strength," was the answer I received through a group of beings calling themselves 'The Lords of Karma'. I had hit a golden vein of hope.

"How? What help?" I asked.

"Draw upon 'The High Priestess'."

Who could this mysterious 'High Priestess' be? So, I wrote to her. Who are you? How can you help me in my life and world?

'The High Priestess' revealed herself to me through daily journaling. I just wrote to her about everything I needed to support me. I asked her to help me and release me from the karmic pattern I had endured unconsciously for so long in my quest to be a 'good woman'.

'The High Priestess' said, "Go to EGYPT! Go with a group. Get a group to go to Egypt with you … now. Now. Now."

I trusted the guidance I received and within two months I had gathered a group together. My flights were paid for, and I was on my way to teach for two weeks on my first teaching tour.

As I stood in front of the great pyramid of Giza for the first time, I felt I was going to physically die from the pain in my heart. My shattered heart reformed itself, magnetising 'The High Priestess's heart energy and finding my own 'lost heart'. Egypt transformed my consciousness and I now embody and teach through the language of the 'One Heart'.

Until I felt the magnetising force that ripped through me, I could not have imagined the power of the force which, when activated, changed me to live through my heart's truth as a multi-dimensional being. To be the embodiment of the 'One Heart' vibration meant I was ready to truly live as this multi-dimensional being, receiving, de-coding, transmitting and speaking the language of the 'One Heart'.

I become an embodiment of 'All' when I live through my intelligent heart.

Who is the transformed one?

You, when you allow yourself to say "YES" to 'The Goddess' within and listen to her.

Be in this allowance: Your heart will love you for it.

You are the 'One Heart' of 'The Mother', you become 'The Remembered One'.

The Truth Behind the Clouds

by Helen Penemenos

"The known of the unknown which we already own."

~Helen Penemenos

The truth sits in a place I will call the 'known of the unknown'. The 'known of the unknown which we already own', is a place behind the clouds where all the information lies and the truth is revealed....

My own experience of departed loved ones include a particular uncle who appeared in my dreams at the same hour, 4am, on many occasions for more than 10 years. He shared valid information with me from the other side, where all is seen, and not only did he expose everything he wanted me to know from that place, he also provided me with protection during certain events that would occur in the future on this side. I am blessed to have experienced this and am grateful for all the learning and support I received from him.

10 years of quality time with this soul helped me to understand on a soul-level who he really was and who I really am. I am who I am, and my spiritual gifts are real. We all have our journeys to complete on this earth, and we mustn't forget we are doubtful human beings, it's in our make-up, and unless we allow the unknown to become known, through the work that's required, we will never see the truth behind the clouds whilst in human form. Is it possible, one may ask? Of course it

is! The messages will appear in different shapes or forms, whether from the deceased or from other sources of evidence.

I have always been spiritual; in fact, I was born knowing that we know the truth that lies deep within us. The answers are there, it's a matter of unfolding what's already there.

The communication with my beloved uncle ended in a way I foresaw. He appeared for the last time in a white robe floating amongst the clouds in a tranquil place, showing me his wrist and pointing at a watch he was wearing. He was communicating with me that it was time to move on. It was a beautiful goodbye; his soul was travelling somewhere else, call it reincarnation or whatever one wants to call it, he was commencing another journey, reassuring me that all would be well and that I was not alone. The soul is omnipresent and his protection would still be with me.

He has departed and I wish him well, but the clouds are still there; the clouds are giving me the answers I seek. Gazing at the clouds is a type of meditation. The answers are received through thoughts, shapes, letters or colours. I share this with you all and my wish for you is that the truth from behind the clouds appears to you with peace and clarity as it has to me in this school called life. Imagine the clouds being your whiteboard of a classroom, filled with all the information you require.

Humble Mentorship

by Irina Gladushchenko

In memory of Fiona

*"Keeping your body healthy is an expression of gratitude
to the whole cosmos – the trees, the clouds, everything."*

-Tich Nhat Hanh

Difficult life crossroads; existential questions; seeking my life purpose....

When I reflect upon the extraordinary time in my life when I changed career from a senior software architect to an energetic healer, and the ten years of transition, I see many smiling faces and many healing hands that supported me along the way. I am forever grateful to all of you, and also to my family and friends. Some of you are still here by my side, a few have disconnected, and there have also been farewells into the spirit world.

All my life I felt a strong desire to find a way to express my inner colours and to find my unique creative outlet but, when the colours and caveman-like drawings started to pour out of me, I was not ready to accept this gift.

Child-like drawings in Bollywood colours were flowing in a constant stream, making me feel puzzled, confronted and curious all at the same time. I had no idea what all of this meant! Was this the unique expression I was waiting for? Really?

After a couple of weeks of overflowing colours, producing strange shapes and trying to make sense of it all, I dared to share them with my husband. Encouraged by him, I also sent a couple of drawings to my mentor. And then the magic began to happen....

My mentor anonymously forwarded these onto his spiritual PA Fiona, who tuned in to each of them. She came back with messages for me, and I'll share just one example that turned my perception about my works, colours and art expression upside down:

"This drawing is showing a magnification of individual cell formation. The artist is visualising the cells inside her body, in this case, inside the uterus.

The spiraling gold light surrounding the cell walls indicates that the blood is immaculate, allowing the blood to carry more light in the blood supply. It is happening throughout the entire body.

The process within the body to convert the positive and negative electrical charge into light energy within the blood and cells happens through the process of photosynthesis.

This process has been activated to perform to a very high vibration. This vibration is outside the normal capacity of the human body.

The texture inside the cells look alive with health and vitality, showing a jewel-like crystal quality.

The cells are radiating golden light, movement and vibration is rapid, and blood supply is in abundance. The cycle of new cell growth is quick and fast, overtaking the old tired cells all over the body.

This body is in a rapid process of renewal and rejuvenation of organs, blood, and cells.

Endocrine and lymphatic systems are working in overdrive to match the performance of the spiritual vessel. Amazing!"

I still remember the feeling after reading this description – attuned, grounded and joyful.

In that moment, my admiration for the human body in general, gratitude to my body systems, and connectedness to other living things went to a whole new level.

A Little Divine Intervention

by Sheila Fawns

"Meditation clears the mind and connects the soul."

~ Sheila Fawns

My favourite meditation centre was closing down. I was upset; I had been teaching meditation there for about three years. I loved the people, I loved the whole atmosphere of the place and my inner child was getting really distraught that she had nowhere to go, nowhere to be with like-minded people. As I was driving to and from my classes, I started to notice all the commercial buildings along the journey that were available for lease. I particularly kept noticing places that were above other commercial premises. Within three weeks, I knew every place along the route that was for lease.

One day I was sitting at my computer and heard a voice in my head say very loudly, "You should look in Jannali". I live about five mins from Jannali and I told that voice, in no uncertain terms, that there was nothing to look at in Jannali. I knew Jannali like the back of my hand and would already know if there was something to lease there. I kept on with my work, had lunch and then went back to my computer. I heard for the second time, a really loud, clear voice say to me, "You should look in Jannali". Again, I told the voice how ridiculous this was, I knew Jannali and there was nothing there! Even though I knew there was nothing I decided I'd have a look anyway. Lo and behold there was a premises for rent! From the outside it looked very similar to my favourite meditation space in Annandale. I knew it was the 'Law of Correspondence' at work. I was shocked to see the rent was well within the amount I wanted to pay, but was still skeptical. I rang the real estate agent and met him there that same afternoon. The space was being used by a courier company and it was a mess; the walls were a lurid green and the carpet was covered in stains. For meditation, we sometimes sit on the floor! But I knew it was big enough to hold workshops, meditation and maybe even some yoga. I knew it was right. We took an 18-month lease which, at the time, I thought would be long enough for a new city meditation centre to open and that I would go to work there. We decorated, replaced the carpet, built a small separate space to prepare for classes, gave it a name – Harmony Centre Sydney South – and we were off. We are still here eight years later!

Today, the 8th August 2020, I taught a meditation and two of the women attendees, with tears in their eyes, said how very grateful they are that they still have this space to come to, how special it is and that it is somewhere they can come to be truly nurtured. COVID-19 had caused them stress, and they really appreciated this space I created.

Truly, the miraculous divine at work, so grateful that I live a life of meaning, what else is there? Really?

For the Love of Passion

by Luke Myers

"Be true to yourself, and you'll be true to everyone."

~ Luke Myers

I was recently thinking about how passionate I once was about almost everything. Things people said or did, to me or to someone else, or to no-one in particular. It occurred to me that my passion had dropped. I wasn't interested in so much anymore. It was concerning that I had lost my passion, my fire, my having an opinion, voicing that opinion, actioning it; it seemed to have evaporated. It troubled me for a while, and I reflected on it without an answer. Perhaps I'd just given up.

I don't think I've travelled the easiest path in life, for a number of reasons that I mostly understand. A difficult childhood, mental health disorders, a bad marriage, a terrible divorce, a co-dependent relationship, losing pretty much everything and having to start again. I recognise that I'm capable of a lot of things; good at some, successful at possibly none. I've never felt successful or capable. I feel that I tried, but the more I tried, the more I failed. And I've reflected on that a lot. Perhaps, I've just given up.

But I'm still excited by music, by learning, by my wife, my daughter, my friends, travel, dancing, experiencing life. I just don't engage as broadly or as deeply as I did. So, I can't have given up. And then it came to me.

A friend posted a video online. It showed a man sitting at a restaurant table calmly eating his meal. Meanwhile, around him, what started as a confrontation rapidly escalated to a melee and then a full brawl. The man sat at the table, calmly eating his meal, occasionally, momentarily, looking up before returning to his food.

A few people commented on the post, mostly about the people, about the violence. Some commented on the man who must have had something wrong with him or been so hungry that he paid no attention to the others, or how good the food must have been that it couldn't be interrupted.

I looked at him and saw me. This wasn't a man who didn't care. This was a man who didn't care about things that didn't matter, that didn't matter to him. It occurred to me that I've had enough trouble in my own life that I don't need to get involved in the trouble in other people's lives. When something doesn't directly impact me, I don't get involved. That someone has an opinion or belief or value different from mine, I don't feel the need to share mine unless it's requested. I don't need to change other people. I don't need to get involved where I don't need to get involved.

I am not calm and peaceful or mindful. I have not reached some level of enlightenment or self-actualisation. In most ways, I'm still the erratic, over-thinking, over-acting person I always have been and probably always will be. I still get excited. I still get passionate. I can still exhaust people with my passion and excitement when it's something I really care about. The only very small, yet immensely huge difference, is that I am passionate about things I care about, things that are important to me.

I have not lost my passion. I have learnt to be passionate about what actually matters.

Temper Tantrums
by Sheila Fawns

"There is no such thing as a perfect parent,
so just be a real one."

– Sue Atkins

Many years ago, I was learning a fabulous energy modality called 'Ignite your Spirit' (IYS). I was learning all about chakras and how they impacted us. I was loving the work and putting it into practice as often as I could. At this time, my daughter was about 12 and coming into those tricky teenage years. She had a mind of her own and wasn't afraid to let me know about it. One day we were in a really bad shouting/arguing match, and I decided to do something different so, as politely as I could at the time, I left her bedroom to let her 'have a look at her behaviour and her attitude'.

I went downstairs into my 'healing room' where I meditate, do spiritual practices and see clients. I decided to use my IYS energy skills and 'energetically swept' the relationship between us. I swept my solar plexus, where the ribs meet, as it is said to be all about us wanting our own way. I swept her solar plexus and then I cut all energetic cords between us that didn't serve us, and finally 'cooled' down the solar plexus energy centre, using another energy technique I had learned called pranic healing – this whole process took about six minutes.

Literally three minutes later she came down the stairs, into my room and apologised for her behaviour and said she had been out of line and it wasn't my fault – she had been grumpy and in a mood and she was sorry she had taken it out on me!

I considered this a minor miracle; if you have teens or pre-teens, you will know what I mean. I used this technique often throughout her teenage years and also with my two sons. I'm so grateful I knew and understood energy healing and what a difference it can make!

How the Book Came into Being

by Jennifer Nurick and Irina Gladushchenko

on behalf of the International Energetic Healing Association (IEHA)

*"The universe buries strange jewels deep within us all,
and then stands back to see if we can find them."*

~ Elizabeth Gilbert

All books go through a birthing process. Some are called into being through the will of an individual, and some float in to be received by the group or the individual. Elizabeth Gilbert's book "Big Magic" talks about this creative process in the most beautiful way.

For our book, the inspiration came in the form of being received. As all projects go through a slightly different process, we thought you might be inspired to hear about the birth and phases of this undertaking.

We can liken the book to carrying and birthing a baby, and the IEHA to being the mother. The process of mothering is different for every pregnancy and for every mother. The journey of the IEHA was one of enormous transformation before the energy of the book could enter.

In transition periods, it is often a time to introspect, to let go, to make space for new energy. For us, this looked like a complete change in the leadership team. This process was intense and emotional, as will be the case now and again with most true relationships. This is the phase of a bushfire that is raging, hot, dry and merciless. This is how we knew the organisation was still alive and fighting for existence. After any fire, there is a stillness and smoldering.

Not until the rains come, and the seeds that are hidden under the earth become activated, will we see the small green shoots reaching out to meet the sun. Reaching out took the form of reconnecting with the community at large to run groups.

The energy for the book came first as "1001 Ways to Ground" in June 2019 during one of the online energetic mentoring sessions with four community members. We had a quiet moment, tuned into the energy of the collective, and then asked which project would be of service to the energy of the collective. This was a bit like the shoots of the sapling starting to grow. When the energy came in for the project, there was an apparent energetic boost for everyone.

After that, there was a shift in the energy team of the IEHA and a transition period. As a group prepares to receive a new project, this is common: the people aligned with the project step forward, and those who are not required, step back for a time. This is where having greater flex and flow in an organisation can be very helpful, rather than fixed roles.

In the new leadership team, there was regularity, commitment and alignment. Everyone was excited about the IEHA and the book. The new team helped to ground the energy of the initiative; other projects were surrendered in the process to focus on the book.

What made us so excited?

- Co-creation was the buzz word
- Faith and trust that our calling to the authors would become a reality
- The gift of stories from the energetic community and beyond
- Addressing the many rich aspects of the human condition
- The sharing of people's most connected experiences helps to move us into more hopefulness, expansiveness and possibility

Our hope for the book:

- That each person reading this book is touched in some way and inspired to connect more deeply in their own way
- For others to be inspired to write their own story
- For it to be an ongoing and dynamic process – to come to 1001 ways to connect
- To be connected to others on their journey

A Gift From Beyond the Veil

by Susie Nelson-Smith

"Divine sound is the cause of all manifestation.
The knower of the mystery of sound knows the
mystery of the whole universe."

~Hazrat Inayat Khan

In 1994 I travelled to Hawaii with my friend Maggie for the first workshop of a two-year commitment to be trained as crystal healing teachers with Katrina Raphaell.

The island of Kauai is known as the Garden Isle and as we drove into the countryside we understood why. To reach our bed and breakfast accommodation we drove past Kapa'a which is near the coast and turned inland towards the Kealia Forest Reserve and deeper into the centre of the island.

It was a moonless night with rain softly falling when Maggie and I entered the warm jacuzzi. We were quiet so as not to disturb the other guests. We placed our crystals and gems around the edge of the jacuzzi, lit our collection of candles and settled in to relax and meditate in the warmth.

I reached out to Maggie and whispered," Oh no, someone has turned on their radio, I can hear music."

Maggie replied, "Susie, I can't hear anything."

"There, there it is again," I said softly. Maggie said, "You must be hearing something from another dimension because there is no sound."

We both settled back into the water and as I relaxed, I began to feel deeply peaceful again. That was when I heard the singing for the second time. It sounded like a choir of a thousand voices. I had not heard sounds like that before. It was not the voice of one person or even the voices of many. It sounded as though a thousand voices were singing together. It was not a song, rather it was like a movement.

Later, when I tried to describe what I had heard to my family and friends, the best way I could explain it was to compare the sound with an image of starlings flying together, in a formation called a murmuration. Even the name "murmuration" helped to explain the sound clearly. It was like a harmonious murmur of vast proportions that felt as though it went on to the depths of infinity.

For a little while I floated on the sound in the warm jacuzzi until I became conscious that I was experiencing something very unusual. With this realisation, I came right back into the third dimension of my body again. My immediate reaction upon realising that I had been listening to a celestial choir was to say, "Thank you God, for this beautiful gift."

My natural extrasensory perception is claircognisant and when I receive visions or heard voices, I believe they are gifts from God. They have been so unexpected. I believe I receive these gifts because of my strong faith in a world beyond our 3-dimensional reality. I have been truly fortunate to receive several gifts of this nature during my life. Each experience has connected me more deeply with the mother, the father, with all – to the Universe in all its magnificent splendour.

The Three Ducks

by Christian Roth

*"A truly wondrous and magical experience while walking
with my dog along the banks of the Yarra River."*

~ Christian Roth

The cold kisses of the wintry morning rain stung my face like frigid,
unemotional pecks from casually passing socialites at a charity luncheon.
I was walking along the leaf-lined path meandering the banks of the
Yarra River in the sleepy little hollow of a town called Warburton. My
faithful companion Angus, a border collie, was walking ahead, tail high
with head cocked listening to my constant venting.

I was angry, frustrated and feeling lost.

The relationship I was in was over and it was time to move on, but
I was afraid. How to start over? I was doubting myself and my worth
as a man, a lover, and a partner. On we walked, my ranting quieted by
the gentle babbling river as it swept over, under and around the rocks
in its path.

I always come to the river when I need to connect, to ground myself
in nature's richness and splendour. Filling my soul with her energy,
feeling the connection, that magical moment when everything around
you stands still and you become interconnected with the all.

Today more than ever I needed that connection.

We came upon a secluded wooden bench nestled under a grove of gum trees where the water was stilled by a tongue-shaped inlet that gently lapped the grassy bank. We sat, Angus next to me, watching the river.

I relaxed my body, calmed my mind, and tried to let go of my cares. My breathing slowed and became rhythmic. I focused on the river, becoming one with its flow. I could sense Angus next to me, his breathing mirroring mine.

Time slowed and we entered that magical interconnected realm.

While in this meditative state three ducks approached from across the river. They paddled up into the inlet and stopped in front of us. Normally, I would have thought they had come for food, but Angus was sitting next to me and ducks and dogs do not mix. Yet here they were, two brown ducks flanking a white duck.

I could sense the ducks were here for a reason. I asked them if they were afraid. The white duck in the middle paddled forward from between the two brown ducks and stopped a few feet away.

Was this a 'no'?

Then I asked if they would help me with some questions and the white duck paddled back between the other two.

Could this mean 'yes'?

I began to ask them questions – some I already knew the answer to. Every time the answer was 'no' the white duck would paddle away from the other two. And when the answer was 'yes' it would paddle back, each time nestling itself between the other two. The two brown ducks never moved.

Entranced, enriched and invigorated with the wonder of this experience, my soul filled with joy and positive energy. I felt alive. Aware of the rain again, I came back into the present. The connection was broken, the moment lost.

We were once again ducks, dog and man.

Angus jumped from the bench. The ducks scurried to the other side of the river. I stood up and stretched. I knew the path I needed to take and what I would do. We started off again and I looked at my watch; over an hour had passed.

I smiled and Angus, trotting ahead, smiled knowingly back.

Who Said That?

by Simonne Lee

"Animals do speak,
but only to those who who choose to listen…"

~ Annonymous

Growing up as an only child my mum made sure I always felt like I had siblings – an animal or two! I had every pet you can think of and my poor mum was ever so patient and loving. I was always talking to my siblings whether they were furry, scaly, feathered, fishy or hard-shelled. I thought it was normal; so normal, that it was not until I was a teenager that I realised most of my friends didn't hear their animals talking back to them. In fact, all my friends thought I was making it up and teased me, so I learnt to keep it to myself.

It wasn't until my mid-20s after moving back to Australia from my travels overseas, that I was adopted by a stray alpha female feline. Her name was Cubby. She completely changed my world and by world, I mean EVERYTHING! My homelife, my career, my way of communicating and how I interacted with animals from that moment onwards was different. It also impacted my human relationships.

This black and white cat taught me the depth and true meaning of animal communication. She taught me that all living beings have a soul and higher consciousness. She taught me how to be descriptive and expressive in our communication. Cubby also showed me how animals can be consciously aware and tap into their own intuition.

During our 10-year relationship (or apprenticeship as she would call it), Cubby guided me in the development of animal communication. We didn't just have basic conversations; we would negotiate on rules and what we expected from each other. Then something happened in the middle of our relationship. I decided to leave my role in the corporate world to start my business. I stepped into the world of animal communication professionally. It was a total leap of faith and challenged many of my own beliefs in trusting that:

1. I could help and make a difference to animals and their families
2. I could create a living out of this crazy passion of mine
3. I wouldn't be abandoned by my peers

I worked on my limiting beliefs and started working with animals and their parents, creating a deeper understanding of what was expected and desired from each other. I was getting results for my clients as there were immediate changes in their pets. Word of mouth spread. So much so, that my clients asked me to teach them how to communicate with their pets. This created a whole new adventure for me – teaching animal communication for beginners and professionals.

I love what I do and feel so lucky to be doing what I am passionate about. I am forever grateful to that black and white cat, Cubby. She rocked my world and guided me into turning my dream into a reality.

Unconditional Love

by Aurélie Hervet

*"The greatest gift that you can give to others is the gift of
unconditional love and acceptance."*

~ Brian Tracy

I could tell you the story of how a cancer scare got me on a self-discovery quest, and got me selling all my possessions, traveling the world
on my own, exploring holistic healing practices, to finally find my
purpose. This is all well and true, but this is only the tip of the iceberg!

Let me tell you about the bigger part, the part under the surface...
those beliefs and patterns of behaviours I learnt from my parents, who
learnt from their parents, who learnt from their parents... running
subconsciously my thoughts, words and deeds.

The strongest belief that runs in my family is unconditional love.

As a matter of fact, I couldn't find any record of divorce in centuries
(I did my family tree). You could object that it doesn't mean they were
all happy marriages, especially in old times when divorce was not an
option. There was indeed a lot of tragedies throughout time, but it was
never for lack of love. In fact, it was quite the opposite.

It's the story of Georgette, my grandmother born in a wealthy family,
who was disinherited for marrying Eugene, a farm boy. Building their

own family, they lived in a bus and saw their 11 children taken away and placed in foster homes. They never saw them again, and Eugene died literally heartbroken (heart attack).

It's the story of 11 sisters and brothers, finding each other again 40 years later, searching in vain for their parents and trying to understand what had happened. They have been celebrating this special bond, with new children, grandchildren and great-grandchildren, every year since.

It's the story of Florence and Jean-Louis, my parents, also from different socioeconomic backgrounds, who demonstrated their love through thick and thin, until he was accepted by my grandparents like a new son.

And so many more incredible stories of trust, respect, vulnerability, and acceptance have conditioned me to believe that love is the most powerful and purest form of healing.

Through all the hardships, and by fighting conventions and societal norms in the most pacific way, my ancestors taught me to forgive, and to always keep an open mind and a compassionate heart. Those causing pain would have been in terrible distress themselves to act the way they did. And, should they have experienced the smallest amount of that special feeling uniting those before me, they would have known that no physical separation would ever set them apart.

I now live in Sydney, millions of kilometres away from my family, and it took me years of travelling, meeting incredible people, learning so much about the world and myself, to find out that the real treasure, the object of my quest, was always with me in the first place... the unconditional love passed on from generation to generation in my family.

I Followed My Dreams

by Yukari Doi

*"You are never too old to set another goal
or to dream a new dream."*

~ C.S Lewis

My name is Yukari, and I am from Osaka, Japan. I always wanted to go overseas and made my first dream come true when I went to the USA. After that, I became an air hostess and travelled all over the world. I knew I would not be satisfied until I worked in a country overseas. This opportunity came in 1991 when I visited a small town in East Gippsland, Victoria. The principal of the school offered me a job, and that is how my life in Australia started. When I first experienced Ultimate Energetic (UE) healing in 2017, I was already a reiki master and therefore understood energy healing. It helped both my physical and emotional state. The experience was life-changing, and it made me want to study this modality.

I went to a UE workshop and began using the healing on myself. This opened me up to my own energy and my higher self. I was receiving messages, and one day I received a message I did not understand. It said, "I want to be a principal." I did not understand why I heard this message within me.

To my surprise, a few weeks after the workshop, I was promoted to Head of Department. But I was still puzzled by the message about becoming a principal. The following year I saw an article on Facebook about starting a primary school in Bali. I decided to enquire about it. I went to Bali to see the school and talk about the opportunity. I was employed, and this opportunity allowed me to live in Bali as a school principal for six months. I found that this experience was hard since I needed to work with Indonesian teachers, international parents and the owner of the school who was Japanese.

What I learnt from this experience was to respect myself, to give myself permission to quit something if it is not what I want, and not to worry about what other people think of me. These three major learnings were there because of my background of being Japanese. I still catch myself being and doing things that do not serve me. It is getting less frequent, but I leant that it is a lifelong experience of confirming who I am and letting go of who I was trained to be.

I am still working on myself every day. I notice how I have changed and what I still need to let go of. What I have learnt from my experience is that dreams will come true if I have clear intentions. I have the power within me to create my future.

The Kingfisher
by Kate Baker

"The true spirit is beautiful and while life is fragile,
it is yet eternal."

~ Kate Baker

Dad was dying.

I met my brothers at a beachside cafe to try to come to terms with a significant decision we'd needed to make. Days earlier dad turned 96 and now we were witnessing a rapid decline. Recovering from a broken hip in rehab, an outbreak of flu at the centre changed everything. The rehab centre told us they could no longer care for his escalating needs and had given us two weeks to find an alternative.

Taking dad home was not a viable option for many reasons. He was confused and not really capable of making informed decisions on his own. We struggled with this as dad had made many wise choices over the past few years and self-autonomy was his most prized value. He was the kind of person who, when he realised he was not cooking nutritious meals for himself, arranged daily meal delivery. When having a tough time hanging bed linen on the washing line, he arranged for his clothes to be laundered. He was proud of these decisions. Now we had had to take this final decision out of his hands and find a nursing home.

It was odd being in this cafe having a meal with only my brothers, as meals with them together had always involved the broader family. We spoke in generalities initially, avoiding the inevitable.

The instant dad was mentioned, a bird flew into the cafe and crashed. Everyone in the cafe gasped. I got up and found a beautiful blue kingfisher with its wings splayed, seemingly dead. Gently gathering its wings, I picked it up. I felt the strongest impulse to take it outside into nature.

As I crouched among the bushes an older woman approached me and said, "This bird is from the spirit realm. Hold it close to your chest. It can easily pass right now, and you must keep it near your heart. When it flutters, you will know it is going to be okay and is ready to be released."

I sat quietly with this beautiful bird as its eyes flickered and it drifted between here and beyond. It seemed the universe was communicating with me about my dad. A feeling of true gentleness and love came over me. After a while, I returned to the cafe, kingfisher at my chest, and we continued our conversation.

Eventually the little bird's wings began to flutter. I asked my brothers if they would help me free our little friend. Crossing the road again, I stroked the kingfisher's wings a little and then held him in the open palm of my hand. He stayed there for many minutes as we spoke to him, we all felt a beautiful connection. Dad was in my mind the whole time. I gently placed our friend on the branch of a nearby tree. He stayed sitting there, near us, for several minutes, in total calmness and trust. Eventually he flew away.

Two weeks later dad passed peacefully. Close friends visited shortly after his passing – their sympathy card had a kingfisher on it. Later I found dad's favourite coffee mug – it had a kingfisher on it too.

My dad had promised to communicate with me from beyond.... Yes, there is only oneness....

Desert Dawn

by Jacquelyn Bushell

"You are 'enough'. In this moment
and every moment, you are always enough."

~ Jacquelyn Bushell

I'm at Mutawintji and the desert stretches out from here for endless miles of red rocks, sand, spinifex and dusty, green mulga trees. The nearest town is Broken Hill, a few hours' drive along a long dirt road to the southwest. Around me are gorges, dry riverbeds, vast red gums and an endless, wide sky. I've been out here a week, camping, walking, sitting and gazing at the Milky Way, a river of light in an ocean of velvet darkness. The timeless stillness and the inherent vitality in this bone-dry place draws me back again and again. In the vast spaciousness, everything in me can find a place to rest, to just be. I come home to something older, wiser and simpler.

One of the things I do is make essences from flowers and rocks. This involves placing an object in a bowl of water, meditating with it and noticing what arises as insight. The water amplifies and imprints the pattern, which can be kept and offered therapeutically. It's a spiritual practice of communion, of sacred oneness.

I pack up and leave before dawn on the winter solstice, driving over a road as bumpy as corrugated iron. The sky is beginning to softly lighten to greys and a blush pink. A few minutes later and the sun emerges, a bright sliver of gold rimming the horizon. I pull over to watch. It inches a little higher, revealing a dazzling light, then suddenly the cockatoos and parrots explode into wakefulness with a cacophony of wild screeches. Thick clouds of them rise up from the trees, wheeling and dancing crazily. Light flows out over the land, casting lengthy shadows behind trees and enflaming the deep red of the ancient rocks. The ridges and gorges here are so old they make the Himalayas look like toddlers in comparison.

Suddenly, a message startles my reverie, "make an essence". Now, I have to admit, I've got a lot of rules about making essences. So, if I was to make one of dawn, I should have been there the night before, calmly meditating and beginning the process well before sunrise. But by now, the sun is halfway up. Make an essence? Absurd! I ignore the message. Then, it comes again. So, against my better judgement, I sit my bowl out in the middle of the road. The sun rises even higher and a vibrant halo of pink, yellow and orange arcs across the sky. The birds are going crazy. The light is incredible, I've never seen a dawn like this before. It's like witnessing the rising of the sun on the very first morning of the earth. I am mesmerised watching this glowing incandescence awakening the desert. Another moment passes and suddenly a river of liquid gold floods down the road, hitting the bowl of water and illuminating it in lustrous radiance. I hold my breath, utterly spellbound.

That's when I hear the words:

It only takes a moment for love to land.

And I know the essence is complete.

Like this beautiful dawn, may you be awakened to the spontaneous power and potential in any moment, illuminated by grace. If you allow it, love is always available. It's as simple as making a choice.

Remember, it only takes a moment for love to land.

Invitation to Write Your Story

The setting for your story

The setting initiates the main backdrop and mood for your story

Introduce your hero/ heroine

The first time we see the main character we should see:

- what's likable/ heroic about them
- what their essential characteristic is

Motivation

There are three major components to motivation:

- activation
- persistence
- intensity

Disruption

The first thing that happens in your story that isn't supposed to happen

Obstacles

- External obstacles are those that are outside of your control
- Internal obstacles are the symptoms of the character's flaws or shortcomings, i.e. of the internal problem

Mentor

A mentor is a character specifically designed to prepare your hero for various obstacles (mental, physical, emotional, or spiritual) they'll face in their journey while achieving their goal.

Quest

A quest is an adventurous journey undertaken by the main character of your story.

Victory

Your victories will inspire!

Learning

Readers can learn from the struggles and celebrate your hero's proudest moments.

Way to Connect

Investing yourself fully into your story and sharing authentic experiences from your heart will build a trusting relationship with your audience.

Enjoy!

Ways To Connect Glossary

Acceptance

"Life is a series of natural and spontaneous changes. Don't resist them; that only creates sorrow. Let reality be reality. Let things flow naturally forward in whatever way they like."

~Lao Tzu

"Healing for Younger Self",
"Taking Responsibility for Your Own Life",
"The Essence of My Heart",
"Unconditional Love",
"How I became 'Great Moon Heart'",
"Van Gogh"

Acknowledgement

"There's a downside to everything, a dark side to everyone, and those who willingly walk in the shadows are a hell of a lot more convincing than those who only acknowledge the sunshine."
~J.M. Darhower, Torture to Her Soul

"Healing for Younger Self",
"How I became 'Great Moon Heart'"

Admiration

"Blessed is he who has learned to admire but not envy, to follow but not imitate, to praise but not flatter, and to lead but not manipulate."
~William Arthur Ward

"Humble Mentorship"

Alignment

"An arrangement in which two or more things are positioned in a straight line or parallel to each other."
~Cambridge Dictionary

"The Phoenix",
"Healing for Younger Self",
"How the Book Came into Being"

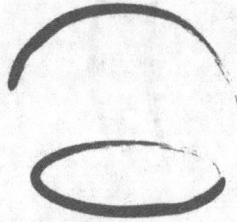

Angels

"Your guardian angel never, ever stops communicating with you.
I feel that at times they should be frustrated with us but they seem to
have endless patience and they never ever give up on us."
~Lorna Byrne, Angels In My Hair

"Born to See",
"Fairies, Readings and Spirit Guides Whispers"

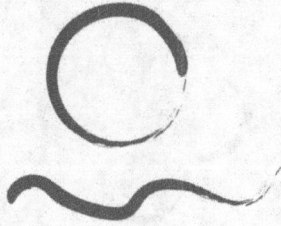

Animal Communication

"Just like individual people, each animal is unique and endowed with different gifts, and some are more spiritually proficient than others. Some are young souls with limited understanding of their mission and purpose, while others have learned spiritual mastery through many lifetimes of experience. All, however, can help us develop fluency in the heart-based language of telepathy."

~Elizabeth Eiler, Swift and Brave: Sacred Souls of Animals

"Who Said That?"

Art

"The principles of true art is not to portray, but to evoke."
~Jerzy Kosinski

"Collaboration over Competition",
"The Creative Block",
"Follow Your Heart",
"Van Gogh",
"Humble Mentorship",
"Connection Within: Refuge in the Body"

Asking Questions

"Judge a man by his questions rather than his answers."
~Voltaire

"The Creative Block",
"A Question or Two"

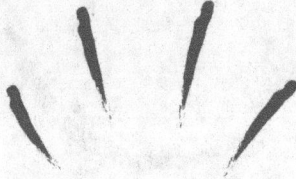

Awakening

"Spiritual awakening is becoming awake to the
aliveness of this moment."
~Eckhart Tolle

"A Story of Hope",
"Wait for the Miracle",
"Sisters",
"Desert Dawn",
"Why I Birthed My Business"

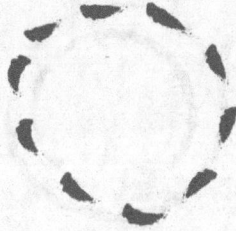

Awareness

"The moment you become aware of the ego in you, it is strictly speaking no longer the ego, but just an old, conditioned mind-pattern. Ego implies unawareness. Awareness and ego cannot coexist."

-Eckhart Tolle

"The Creative Block",
"Meditation – It's all about the Cake",
"Teacher Aniri",
"The Essence of My Heart",
"The Breath",
"Van Gogh",
"A Question or Two",
"For the Love of Passion",
"The Three Ducks",
"Who Said That?"

Beauty

"Everything has its beauty, but not everyone sees it."
~Confucius

"Follow Your Heart",
"Taking Responsibility for Your Own Life",
"Energy of Synchronicity",
"I See Hearts",
"The Essence of My Heart",
"Wait for the Miracle",
"Van Gogh",
"Connection Within: Refuge in the Body",
"Living Buddhas",
"Sisters",
"A Gift From Beyond the Veil",
"The Kingfisher"

Bereavement

"Don't grieve. Anything you lose comes around in another form."
~Rumi

"Life Goes on",
"She Listens Still",
"Taking Responsibility for Your Own Life"

Birth

"Birth is not only about making babies. Birth is about making mothers–strong, competent, capable mothers who trust themselves and know their inner strength."
~Barbara Katz Rothman

"The Phoenix",
"Embracing Resilience",
"She Listens Still",
"Bone Woman ~ Shamanic Mystic",
"How the Book Came into Being"

Birthing

"Birth is an opportunity to transcend. To rise above what we are accustomed to, reach deeper inside ourselves than we are familiar with, and to see not only what we are truly made of, but the strength we can access in and through birth."

~Marcie Macari

"The Phoenix",
"She Listens Still",
"Whale Story",
"Why I Birthed My Business",
"How the Book Came into Being"

Blessing

"When I started counting my blessings, my
whole life turned around."
~Willie Nelson

"Life Goes on",
"Food for the Soul, Body, and Mind",
"Passageways",
"Modern Blessing of Ancient Wisdom",
"A Gift From Beyond the Veil"

Body Wisdom

"I dive into the well of my body, and end up in another world, everything I need, already exists in me, there is no need to look anywhere else."
~Rupi Kaur, Home Body

"The Power of Tuning in",
"'Landing' with Love",
"Whale Story",
"Connection Within: Refuge in the Body",
"Bone Woman ~ Shamanic Mystic"

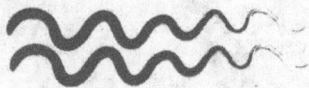

~~~~~

Breath

"If you had to choose between a million dollars
and your next breath, what would you choose?"

~Himalayan Saint

"I See Hearts",
"The Essence of My Heart",
"Passageways",
"How I became 'Great Moon Heart'",
"Van Gogh",
"The Three Ducks",
"Desert Dawn",
"The Breath"

~

Calm

"Calm mind brings inner strength and self-confidence, so that's very important for good health."
~Dalai Lama

"Meditation – It's all about the Cake",
"Finding God on the Cricket Pitch",
"Whale Story"

Changing Limiting Beliefs

"Courage is your natural setting. You do not need to become courageous, but rather peel back the layers of self-protective, limiting beliefs that keep you small."
~Vironika Tugaleva

"Healing for Younger Self"

Co-Creation

"The world we live in is a co-creation, a manifestation of individual consciousness woven into a collective dream. How we are with each other as individuals, as groups, as nations and tribes, is what shapes that dream."

~Oriah Mountain Dreamer

"Collaboration over Competition",
"Energy of Synchronicity",
"How the Book came into Being",
"Why I Birthed My Business"

Collaboration

"When you need to innovate, you need to collaborate."
-Marissa Mayer

"Collaboration over Competition",
"Energy of Synchronicity"

Common Goals

"When people work towards a common goal, they are driven, passionate and purposeful."
~Richard Branson

"Lessons Learnt Along the Way"

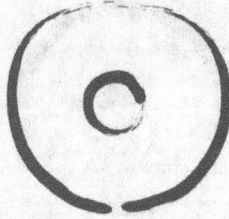

Communication

"The biggest communication problem
is we do not listen to understand.
We listen to reply."
~Stephen R. Covey

"Collaboration over Competition",
"The Creative Block",
"Who Said That?"

Community

"Building community is to the collective
as spiritual practice is to the individual."
~Grace Lee Boggs

"A Little Divine Intervention",
"How the Book Came into Being"

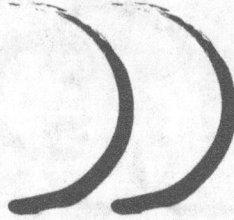

Connecting with Spirits

"My religion consists of a humble admiration of the illimitable superior spirit who reveals himself in the slight details we are able to perceive with our frail and feeble mind."
~Albert Einstein

"Life Goes on",
"Why I Birthed My Business"

Contemplation

"Contemplation is the highest form of activity."
~Aristotle

"The Essence of My Heart"

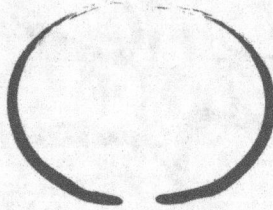

Conversation

"A man's character may be learned from the adjectives which he
habitually uses in conversation."
-Mark Twain

"Meditation — It's all about the Cake",
"A Story of Hope",
"The Essence of My Heart",
"Shadow",
"Who Said That?",
"Unconditional Love",
"The Kingfisher"

Core Memory

"A core memory is a memory attached to a momentous point in your life, that plays a part in your character or personality from that point on."
~Laura Hamblyn

"Healing for Younger Self"

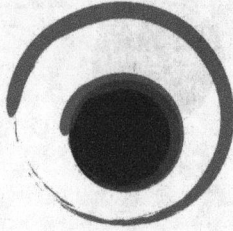

Core Values

"If you compromise your core values, you go nowhere."
-Roy T. Bennett

"The Creative Block",
"For the Love of Passion"

Creative Expression

"It is the supreme art of the teacher to awaken joy in creative expression and knowledge."

-Albert Einstein

"Teacher Aniri",
"Humble Mentorship"

Creative Pursuits

"Creativity is intelligence having fun."
~Albert Einstein

"How the Book came into Being"

Creativity

"Create. Not for the money. Not for the fame. Not for the recognition. But for the pure joy of creating something and sharing it."

~Ernest Barbaric

"Collaboration over Competition",
"Follow Your Heart",
"Van Gogh",
"How the Book Came into Being",
"A Gift From Beyond the Veil",
"Why I Birthed My Business"

Divine

"The eyes of the soul of the multitudes are unable to endure
the vision of the divine."
~Plato

"Energy of Synchronicity",
"I See Hearts",
"The Essence of My Heart",
"Passageways",
"Wait for the Miracle",
"Bone Woman ~ Shamanic Mystic",
"Why I Birthed My Business",
"A Little Divine Intervention"

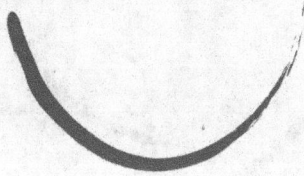

Divine Feminine

"She has risen, she has fully opened her heart. She knows her power and has stepped into it. She will not conform or play small. She is wild, playful and free. She lives with passion and creativity. She knows who she is. She is wisdom, she is magical, she is pure love, she is beautiful. She is Divine Feminine and she is unstoppable."
~Lisa Marie Wright

"Living Buddhas",
"Finding 'The Mother'"

Divine Help

"The difficulty is solved with divine help."
-Lailah Gifty Akita

"Whale Story"

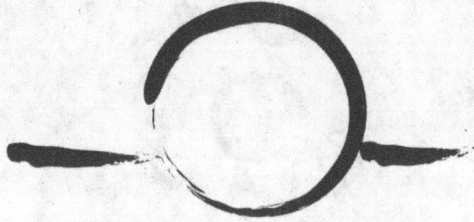

Divine Masculine

"An awakened man is a warrior of the heart.... He calls to other conscious men to join the revolution, lay down their ego, and with true masculine energy demonstrates what it means to return love. ..."
~Daniel Nielsen

"Finding 'The Mother'"

Divinity within

"Treat everyone you meet like God in drag."
~Ram Das

"I See Hearts"

Earth Wisdom

"Nature is painting for us, day after day, pictures of infinite beauty."
~John Ruskin

"Desert Dawn"

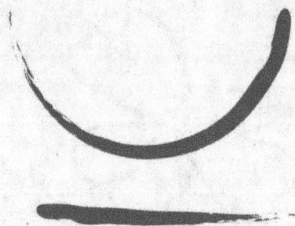

Emotional Healing

"If you want to fly, give up everything that weighs you down."
~Buddha

"Connection Within: Refuge in the Body"

Emotional Intelligence

"Emotional intelligence is your ability to recognize and understand emotions in yourself and others, and your ability to use this awareness to manage your behavior and relationships."
~Travis Bradberry

"The Power of Tuning in"

Energy

"Life is energy and, as such, it belongs to all,
reaches all, and blesses all."
~Donna Goddard, The Love of Devotion

"Meditation – It's all about the Cake",
"Trust the Connection",
"Energy of Synchronicity",
"I See Hearts",
"Whale Story",
"Shadow",
"The Breath",
"How I became 'Great Moon Heart'",
"A Little Divine Intervention",
"How the Book Came into Being",
"The Three Ducks",
"The Kingfisher"

Energy Work

"Energy work uses universal energy and the energy of the client to effect positive change in the client."
~Jennifer Nurick

"Shadow",
"Temper Tantrums"

Enlightenment

"The word enlightenment conjures up the idea of some superhuman accomplishment, and the ego likes to keep it that way, but it is simply your natural state of oneness with Being."
~Eckhart Tolle

"How I became 'Great Moon Heart'"

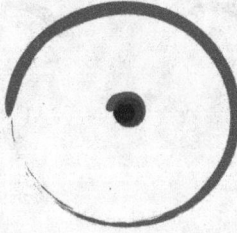

Essence

"The core nature of something that may in its fullness feel abstract."
~Jennifer Nurick

"Teacher Aniri",
"The Essence of My Heart",
"A Turning Point",
"Wait for the Miracle",
"Desert Dawn"

Exploration

"Exploration is really the essence of the human spirit."
~Frank Borman

"Energy of Synchronicity",
"Unconditional Love"

Facing Fears

"Each of us must confront our own fears, must come face to face with them. How we handle our fears will determine where we go with the rest of our lives. To experience adventure or to be limited by the fear of it."

-Judy Blume

"Shadow",
"Why I Birthed My Business"

Faith

"Faith in action is love, and love in action is service."
~Mother Theresa

"Finding God on the Cricket Pitch",
"A Story of Hope",
"Wait for the Miracle",
"Sisters",
"How the Book Came into Being",
"Who Said That?"

Family

"Being genetically related doesn't make you family. Love, support, trust, sacrifice, honesty, acceptance, protection, security, compromise, gratitude, respect and loyalty are what make you FAMILY."

~Tiny Buddha

"Embracing Resilience",
"The Creative Block",
"She Listens Still",
"Energy of Synchronicity",
"A Story of Hope",
"Coming Home",
"Sisters",
"Signposts for Life",
"A Little Divine Intervention",
"Temper Tantrums",
"Unconditional Love",
"The Kingfisher"

Father Sky

*"The complementary marriage of Earth Mother and Father Sky,
representing the limitless aspect of Source."*
~Jennifer Nurick

"How I became 'Great Moon Heart'"

Fluidity

"To be able to change state easily."
~Jennifer Nurick

"Collaboration over Competition"

Forgiveness

"If we really want to love we must learn how to forgive."
~Mother Theresa

"Darkness to Light",
"Wait for the Miracle",
"Unconditional Love"

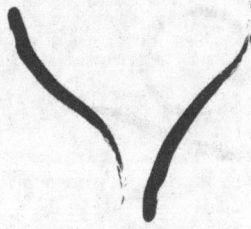

Generosity

"The most generous people are those that give without remembering
and receive without forgetting."
~Unknown

"A Conscious Path",
"Food for the Soul, Body, and Mind",
"Connection Within: Refuge in the Body"

Gentleness

"Be like water; soft as it is, it breaks through rocks
and impenetrable surfaces."
~Matshona Dhliwayo

"Teacher Aniri",
"The Kingfisher"

Going within

"Going within is the process of taking time to check in with yourself, to discover your needs and deep inner guidance."
~Jennifer Nurick

"Darkness to Light",
"Why I Birthed My Business"

Gratitude

"Gratitude is the healthiest of all human emotions. The more you express gratitude for what you have, the more likely you will have even more to express gratitude for."

~Zig Ziglar

"Energy of Synchronicity",
"I See Hearts",
"The Essence of My Heart",
"A Turning Point",
"The Breath",
"How I became 'Great Moon Heart'",
"Van Gogh",
"Living Buddhas",
"Humble Mentorship",
"A Little Divine Intervention",
"Who Said That?"

Grounding

"Love is the grounding of our existence as humans and is the basic emotioning in our systemic identity as human beings."
-Humberto Maturana

"Humble Mentorship"

Growth

"Change is not a bolt of lightning that arrives with a zap.
It is a bridge built brick by brick, every day, with sweat and
humility and slips. It is hard work, and slow work, but it can be
thrilling to watch it take shape."
~Sarah Hepola

"Collaboration over Competition",
"Taking Responsibility for Your Own Life",
"Bone Woman ~ Shamanic Mystic"

Guidance

"Being open to the guidance of your own true Nature will
free others to do the same."
~Wayne Dyer

"Meditation – It's all about the Cake",
"Why I Birthed My Business"

Harmony

"The more in harmony you are with the flow of existence, the more magical life becomes."

~Adyashanti

"The Essence of My Heart",
"Modern Blessing of Ancient Wisdom",
"A Little Divine Intervention"

Healing

"The soul always knows what to do to heal itself. The
challenge is to silence the mind."

~Caroline Myss

"Darkness to Light", "Trust the Connection",
"Meditation – It's all about the Cake",
"Taking Responsibility for Your Own Life",
"Teacher Aniri", "Waiting for Love",
"Finding God on the Cricket Pitch",
"The Essence of My Heart", "Van Gogh",
"Shadow", "Passageways", "Wait for the Miracle",
"Temper Tantrums", "How I became 'Great Moon Heart'",
"Coming Home", "Humble Mentorship",
"A Little Divine Intervention",
"Unconditional Love", "I Followed my Dreams"

Healing Session

"A healing session uses universal energy and the energy of the client to effect positive change in the client."

-Jennifer Nurick

"The Phoenix",
"Meditation — It's all about the Cake",
"Taking Responsibility for Your Own Life",
"Dance of Life",
"Unconditional Love"

High Priestess

"Who is She? She is your power, your Feminine source. Big Mama.
The Goddess. The Great Mystery. The web-weaver. The life force."
~Lucy H. Pearce, Burning Woman

"Finding 'The Mother'"

Higher Guidance

"Faith in the guidance of Spirit gives you the courage to take risks, because you're assured that whatever happens, a Higher Power is on your side and you will survive."
~Colette Baron Reid

"The Power of Tuning in",
"The Creative Block",
"Life Goes on",
"She Listens Still",
"Meditation – It's all about the Cake",
"Taking Responsibility for Your Own Life",
"A Conscious Path",
"Passageways",
"Born to See",
"Fairies, Readings and Spirit Guides Whispers",
"Coming Home",
"Finding 'The Mother'",
"A Gift From Beyond the Veil",
"The Three Ducks",
"Who Said That?",
"Why I Birthed My Business"

Higher Self

"Remember, you don't become a spirit when you die. You already ARE a spirit – right here and now. Whilst on Earth, you also have a body and a soul. Take time to be still and listen to your higher self. The YOU that is connected at all times to Source. That's who you truly are. A magnificent being of energy, light and love. You're amazing."

~Anonymous

"Teacher Aniri",
"Passageways",
"Coming Home",
"Why I Birthed My Business"

Honesty

"As I have said, the first thing is, to be honest with yourself.
You can never have an impact on society if you have not
changed yourself... Great peacemakers are all people of integrity,
of honesty, but humility."
~Nelson Mandela

"Why I Birthed My Business"

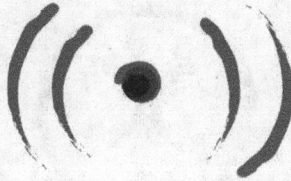

Inner Child

"The inner child lives within all of us, it's the part of us that feels emotions and is playful, intuitive and creative."
~Lucia Capacchione

"A Little Divine Intervention"

Inner Guidance

"Our inner guidance comes to us through our feelings and body wisdom first - not through intellectual understanding. The intellect works best in service to our intuition, our inner guidance, soul, God or higher power - whichever term we choose for the spiritual energy that animates life."
~Dr Christiane Northrup

"How I became 'Great Moon Heart'",
"Signposts for Life",
"Desert Dawn",
"The Power of Tuning in",
"Coming Home",
"Why I Birthed My Business"

Inner Resonance

"Prayer is inner resonance and a capacity for mutuality."
-Richard Rohr

"I See Hearts"

Inner Strength

"Look well into yourself; there is a source of strength which will always spring up if you will always look."
~Marcus Aurelius

"Embracing Resilience",
"Why I Birthed My Business"

• • •

Intention Setting

"Our intention creates our reality."
~Wayne Dyer

"I See Hearts",
"Van Gogh",
"I Followed my Dreams"

Intimacy

"Intimacy is not purely physical. It's the act of connecting with someone so deeply, you feel like you can see into their soul."
~Reshall Varsos

"Teacher Aniri",
"Waiting for Love"

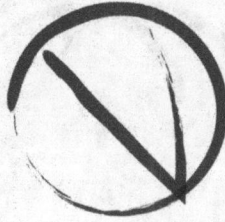

Intuition

"Follow your instincts. That's where true wisdom manifests itself."
-Oprah Winfrey

"The Power of Tuning in",
"The Creative Block",
"Food for the Soul, Body, and Mind", "I See Hearts",
"The Essence of My Heart",
"A Turning Point",
"Born to See",
"How I became 'Great Moon Heart'",
"Fairies, Readings and Spirit Guides Whispers",
"A Question or Two",
"Signposts for Life",
"Who Said That?"

Kindness

"Kindness in words creates confidence. Kindness in thinking creates profoundness. Kindness in giving creates love."
~Lao Tzu

"Follow Your Heart",
"A Conscious Path",
"Connection Within: Refuge in the Body",
"Who Said That?"

Knowing

"Knowing yourself is the beginning of all wisdom."
-Aristotle

"The Truth Behind the Clouds",
"A Little Divine Intervention"

Language of Colours

"Can we consider colour as a language? Colours are beyond words and communicate with us at a deeper level. Colour is a language, through which we perceive the world better."
~Ankita Mishra

"Trust the Connection",
"Humble Mentorship"

Leap

"Sometimes your only transportation is a leap of faith."
~Margaret Shepard

"A Turning Point",
"Who Said That?"

Learning Something New

"When you talk, you are only repeating something you know. But if you listen, you may learn something new."

~Dalai Lama

"Collaboration over Competition",
"The Essence of My Heart",
"The Truth Behind the Clouds"

Letting Go

"Letting go means to come to the realization that some people are a
part of your history, but not a part of your destiny."
~Steve Maraboli

"Bone Woman ~ Shamanic Mystic",
"I Followed my Dreams"

Life after Death

"Seeing death as the end of life is like seeing the horizon
as the end of the ocean."
~David Searles

"Life Goes on"

Life Force Energy

"Life Force energy is the primary energy that sustains all life. Qi / Chi is the foundation of some Eastern Systems, Prana has origins from India, Ki in Japan, Shakti in Hindu, Mana from Polynesia, Nyama from West Africa, Aura from Russia, Chu'Lel origins is from Mayan civilization. The Dreamtime from Aboriginal tribes and many more terms for this Universal Life Force energy within all of us."
~Anastasia Giovanoglou

"I See Hearts"

Light Bearer

"Connection to the Light is a part of Human Design.
Embodying the Light is a Mastery."
-Irina Gladushchenko

"Shadow"

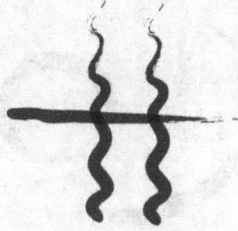

Light Grid

"The light grid is a way to harness the energy in speed Indic patterns
attuned to a particular energy quality, frequency and vibration."
~Luca Orlandi

"Shadow"

Listening

"The first act of love is to listen."
-Paul Tillich

"The Essence of My Heart",
"The Three Ducks"

Listening to Oneself

"There is something in every one of you that waits and listens for the sound of the genuine in yourself. It is the only true guide you will ever have. And if you cannot hear it, you will all of your life spend your days on the ends of strings that somebody else pulls."

~Howard Thurman

"The Power of Tuning in",
"Why I Birthed My Business"

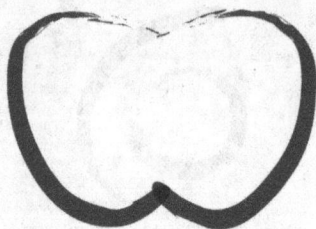

Love

"You are loved just for being who you are, just for existing. You don't have to do anything to earn it. Your shortcomings, your lack of self-esteem, physical perfection, or social and economic success - none of that matters. No one can take this love away from you, and it will always be here."

~Ram Dass

"Life Goes on", "Allowing Adversity to Create Good Change",
"Follow Your Heart", "Taking Responsibility for Your Own Life",
"Teacher Aniri", "Energy of Synchronicity",
"'Landing' with Love", "A Story of Hope",
"Waiting for Love", "Food for the Soul, Body, and Mind",
"Dance of Life", "I See Hearts",
"The Essence of My Heart", "Whale Story",
"Shadow", "Passageways", "Wait for the Miracle",
"Van Gogh", "Connection Within: Refuge in the Body",
"Bone Woman ~ Shamanic Mystic", "Coming Home",
"Sisters", "Finding 'The Mother'", "Who Said That?",
"Unconditional Love", "The Kingfisher", "Desert Dawn"

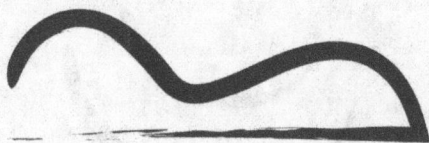

Meditation

"One of the things that meditation teaches us, when we slowly descend into ourselves, is that the sense of peace already exists in us."
~Dalai Lama

"Life Goes on",
"Meditation – It's all about the Cake",
"Allowing Adversity to Create Good Change",
"Trust the Connection",
"Finding God on the Cricket Pitch",
"Dance of Life", "I See Hearts", "Passageways",
"How I became 'Great Moon Heart'",
"Van Gogh", "Living Buddhas", "Coming Home",
"Why I Birthed My Business", "A Question or Two",
"A Little Divine Intervention",
"A Gift From Beyond the Veil",
"The Three Ducks",
"Desert Dawn"

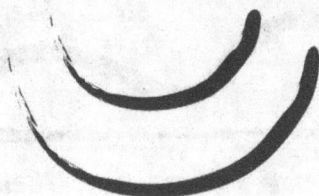

Mental Wellbeing

"Mental health is not just the absence of mental disorder. It is defined as a state of well-being in which every individual realizes his or her own potential, can cope with the normal stresses of life, can work productively and fruitfully, and is able to make a contribution to her or his community."
~World Health Organisation

"Darkness to Light",
"For the Love of Passion"

Mind-Body-Spirit Connection

"When mind, body and spirit are in harmony,
happiness is the natural result."
~Deepak Chopra

"The Essence of My Heart",
"Why I Birthed My Business"
"Coming Home"

Mindfulness

"Mindfulness helps you fall in love with the ordinary."
~Thich Nhat Hanh

The Essence of My Heart",
"The Breath",
"Connection Within: Refuge in the Body"

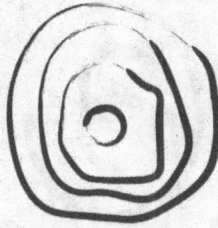

Mother Earth

"We call our Earth by so many names – Mother Earth, Gaia, Earth Mother, Great Mother, Magna Mater, Mother Goddess, Sophia, Mother Nature, Pachamama – it is the homeplace of where we are born, and she is the Mother of all living organisms."
~Anastasia Giovanoglou

"How I became 'Great Moon Heart'"

Mother Nature

"Mother Nature (also known as Mother Earth) can be considered as
the force that controls the weather and all living things and beings –
the source and guiding force of creation."
–Anastasia Giovanoglou

"I See Hearts"

Multidimensional Reality

"Our body is a doorway to our multidimensional magnificence.
When we move our awareness beyond time and space, we can access
any realm where our consciousness resides."

~Peter Smith, Quantum Consciousness:
Journey Through Other Realms

"She Listens Still",
"Energy of Synchronicity",
"Fairies, Readings and Spirit Guides Whispers",
"Finding 'The Mother'",
"A Gift From Beyond the Veil",
"The Kingfisher",
"Why I Birthed My Business"

Nature

"In nature, nothing is perfect and everything is perfect. Trees can be contorted, bent in weird ways, and they're still beautiful."

-Alice Walker

"Collaboration over Competition",
"Allowing Adversity to Create Good Change",
"Follow Your Heart",
"'Landing' with Love",
"I See Hearts",
"Whale Story",
"Shadow",
"Born to See",
"How I became 'Great Moon Heart'",
"Living Buddhas",
"The Three Ducks",
"Who Said That?",
"The Kingfisher",
"Desert Dawn"

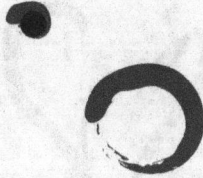

New Culture

"A new culture is defined by the practice of new
ideas and social practices."
~Jennifer Nurick

"Finding 'The Mother'"

New Experiences

"The only source of knowledge is experience."
~Albert Einstein

"How I became 'Great Moon Heart'"

New Possibilities

"Man often becomes what he believes himself to be. If I keep on saying to myself that I cannot do a certain thing, it is possible that I may end by really becoming incapable of doing it. On the contrary, if I have the belief that I can do it, I shall surely acquire the capacity to do it even if I may not have it at the beginning."

~Mahatma Gandhi

"The Creative Block",
"Why I Birthed My Business"

Nurture

"We nurture something while it is still growing with love, we protect it and care for it, so that it may become the fullest version of itself."

-Jennifer Nurick

"Meditation – It's all about the Cake",
"How I became 'Great Moon Heart'",
"A Little Divine Intervention"

One Heart

"One heart, one love, one destiny."
-Bob Marley

"Finding 'The Mother'"

Oneness

"People normally cut reality into compartments, and so are unable to see the interdependence of all phenomena. To see one in all and all in one is to break through the great barrier which narrows one's perception of reality."
~Tich Nhat Hanh

"Finding 'The Mother'"

Parallel Universe

"A parallel universe is a world thought to exist alongside our world with many similarities but being fundamentally different."
~Jennifer Nurick

"Shadow"

Parenting

"There is no such thing as a perfect parent, so just be a real one."
~Sue Atkins

"Passageways",
"Temper Tantrums"

Personal Development

"Life is growth. If we stop growing technically and
spiritually, we are as good as dead."
~Morihei Ueshiba

"Darkness to Light",
"A Conscious Path"

Pilgrimage

"Pilgrimage is a powerful metaphor for any journey with the purpose
of finding something that matters deeply to the traveler."
~Phil Cousineau

"How I became 'Great Moon Heart'",
"Van Gogh"

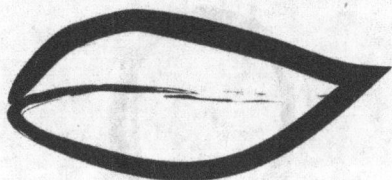

Plant Medicine

"Mother Earth's medicine chest is full of healing
herbs of incomparable worth."
~Robin Rose Bennet

"I See Hearts"

Portal

"A doorway or space leading to another place in time, space."
-Jennifer Nurick

"Shadow",
"Why I Birthed My Business"

Prayer

"Prayer is simply a two-way conversation between you and God."
~Billy Graham

"'Landing' with Love",
"Waiting for Love",
"I See Hearts",
"The Essence of My Heart",
"Shadow",
"Born to See",
"Wait for the Miracle",
"Living Buddhas"
"Coming Home"

Presence

"Presence is a state of inner consciousness."
~Eckhart Tolle

"Teacher Aniri",
"Coming Home",
"Fairies, Readings and Spirit Guides Whispers"

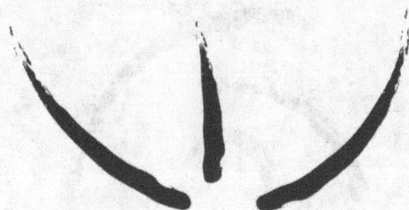

Quality of Life

"Our job is improving the quality of life, not just delaying death."
~Robin Williams

"Meditation – It's all about the Cake"

Random Act of Kindness

"Carry out random acts of kindness, with no expectation of reward, safe in the knowledge that one day someone might do the same for you."
-Princess Diana

"Van Gogh"

Rebirth

"Each night, when I go to sleep, I die. And the
next morning, I am reborn."
~Mahatma Gandhi

"The Phoenix",
"Teacher Aniri",
"Taking Responsibility for Your Own Life",
"A Story of Hope",
"Passageways",
"Connection Within: Refuge in the Body",
"Bone Woman ~ Shamanic Mystic",
"Finding 'The Mother'",
"Sisters",
"Why I Birthed My Business"

Rediscovering

"I invent nothing, I rediscover."
~Auguste Rodin

"Sisters"

Reflection

"Self-reflection is the school of wisdom."
~Baltasar Gracian

"How I became 'Great Moon Heart'",
"Humble Mentorship",
"For the Love of Passion"

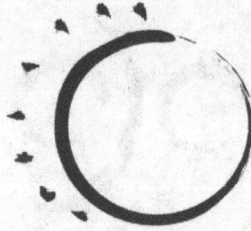

Remembering

"Can you remember who you were before the world
told you who you should be?"
~Charles Bukowski

"Taking Responsibility for Your Own Life",
"Wait for the Miracle",
"Bone Woman ~ Shamanic Mystic",
"Sisters",
"Finding 'The Mother'",
"Coming Home",
"Why I Birthed My Business"

Resonance

"There's a resonance inside us, a sense of who we are. We're a multi-bodied traveler. We're an essence. We're a feeling, an awareness that has an ancient existence."
~Frederick Lenz

"Energy of Synchronicity"

Resourcefulness

"Be positive, be strong and be resourceful. The world
really is what you make of it."
~Bear Grylls

"Follow Your Heart",
"Why I Birthed My Business"

Respect

"Respect is one of the greatest expressions of love."
-Miguel Angel Ruiz

"Healing for Younger Self",
"A Story of Hope",
"I See Hearts",
"Shadow",
"Van Gogh",
"Sisters",
"I Followed my Dreams"

Satsang

"Satsang is the invitation to step into the fire of self-discovery. This fire will not burn you, it will only burn what you are not."
~Mooji

"A Little Divine Intervention"

Self-care

"An empty lantern provides no light. Self-care is the fuel that allows
your light to shine brightly."
~Anonymous

"Coming Home"

Self-discovery

"I understood myself only after I had destroyed myself. And only in
the process of fixing myself, did I know who I really was."
~Sade Andria Zabala

"A Conscious Path",
"A Story of Hope",
"Why I Birthed My Business"

Self-love

"Self-love means having a high regard for your own well-being and
How you love yourself is how you teach others to love you."

~Rupi Kaur

"Healing for Younger Self",
"Follow Your Heart",
"A Story of Hope",
"Coming Home",
"Sisters",
"Finding 'The Mother'"

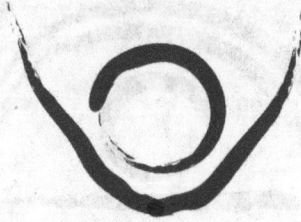

Service

"The best way to find yourself is to lose yourself
in the service of others."
~Mahatma Gandhi

"Wait for the Miracle",
"Modern Blessing of Ancient Wisdom",
"Why I Birthed My Business"

Sharing

"Thousands of candles can be lit from a single candle, and the life of the candle will not be shortened. Happiness never decreases by being shared."
~Buddha

"Collaboration over Competition",
"Teacher Aniri",
"A Story of Hope",
"Food for the Soul, Body, and Mind",
"The Essence of My Heart",
"A Turning Point",
"Sisters"

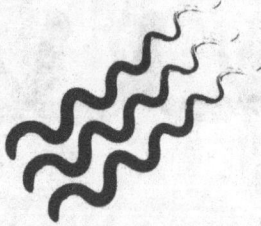

Signs

"You won't miss a sign from the universe. It will keep getting louder and louder until you hear it."
~The Minds Journal

"Life Goes on",
"Trust the Connection",
"I See Hearts",
"Fairies, Readings and Spirit Guides Whispers"
"Coming Home"

Soul

"The soul is not ruled by time or space. The soul is infinite. It blends with the one infinity."

~Ram Das

"The Power of Tuning in",
"Meditation – It's all about the Cake",
"Finding God on the Cricket Pitch",
"Dance of Life",
"The Song of Healing",
"Passageways",
"Coming Home",
"Connection Within: Refuge in the Body",
"The Truth Behind the Clouds",
"A Little Divine Intervention",
"Who Said That?"

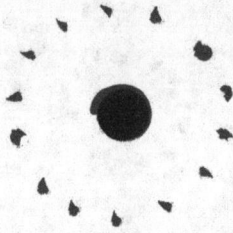

Soul Essence

"Our soul is the sacred essence within us; our deepest purpose. Our unique meaning, the guiding force behind our individual lives."
~Mateo Sol

"I See Hearts"

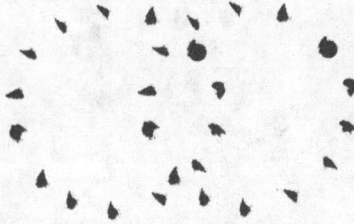

Soul Searching

"The wise use of intelligence required more than academic intelligence; we need soul-searching and deep reflection to live a more balanced and meaningful life."
~Paul TP Wong

"The Creative Block",
"Why I Birthed My Business"

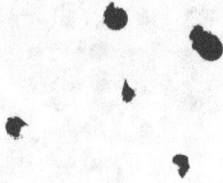

Space

"Space is for everybody. It's not just for a few people in science or math, or for a select group of astronauts. That's our new frontier out there, and it's everybody's business to know about space."
~Christa McAuliffe

"Meditation – It's all about the Cake",
"A Little Divine Intervention"

Spiritual Being

"We are not human beings having a spiritual experience. We are spiritual beings having a human experience."
~Pierre Teilhard de Chardin

"The Power of Tuning in",
"Energy of Synchronicity",
"The Essence of My Heart",
"Passageways",
"Wait for the Miracle",
"Why I Birthed My Business",
"The Three Ducks",
"The Kingfisher"

Stillness

"In the inner stillness where meditation leads, the Spirit secretly anoints the soul and heals our deepest wounds."

~John of the Cross

"I See Hearts",
"The Essence of My Heart",
"The Song of Healing",
"How the Book Came into Being",
"The Three Ducks",
"Desert Dawn"

Studies

"It is a mistake to think that the practice of my art has become easy to me. I assure you, dear friend, no one has given so much care to the study of composition as I."
~Wolfgang Amadeus Mozart

"Modern Blessing of Ancient Wisdom"

Surrender

"Surrender to what is
Let go of what was.
Have faith in what will be."
~Sonia Ricotti

"The Phoenix",
"Bone Woman ~ Shamanic Mystic",
"Why I Birthed My Business"

Synchronicity

"Synchronicity is an ever present reality for
those who have eyes to see."
-Carl Jung

"Energy of Synchronicity",
"I See Hearts",
"Fairies, Readings and Spirit Guides Whispers"

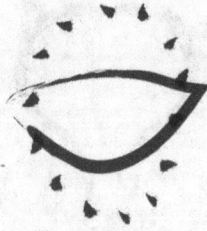

Third Eye

"This one true eye, it beckons me;
To visualise what you can not see.
To escape our bodies, fleshy dense,
is what I know as common sense.
Knowledge continues to multiply,
as I come to understand my third eye."
~Emma Mills

"I See Hearts"

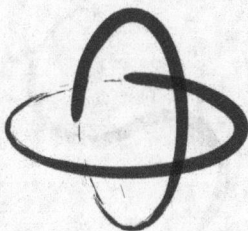

Timelessness

"If one understands eternity as timelessness, and not as an unending timespan, then whoever lives in the present lives for all time."
~Ludwig Wittgenstein

"Life Goes on",
"Passageways",
"Desert Dawn"

Travel

"Travel not to find yourself but remember who you were all along."
-Anonymous

"The Creative Block",
"A Turning Point",
"Whale Story",
"Connection Within: Refuge in the Body",
"Modern Blessing of Ancient Wisdom",
"Who Said That?",
"Unconditional Love",
"I Followed my Dreams"

Trust

"When I live and act from a place of spiritual alignment, I can
TRUST that everything is working out for me, even if I don't know
when or how it will happen."
~Gabrielle Bernstein

"The Phoenix",
"Healing for Younger Self",
"Trust the Connection",
"A Story of Hope",
"I See Hearts",
"The Essence of My Heart",
"Sisters",
"A Question or Two",
"Signposts for Life",
"Who Said That?",
"Finding 'The Mother'"

Truth

"Three things cannot be long hidden: the sun,
the moon, and the truth."
~Buddha

"Follow Your Heart",
"The Essence of My Heart",
"Passageways",
"Why I Birthed My Business",
"The Truth Behind the Clouds"

Tuning in

"When I'm tuned into the energy of
Abundance, I become abundant."
~Gabrielle Bernstein

"The Power of Tuning in",
"A Question or Two"

Tuning into Feelings

"The life of expression is the tuning fork by which we
find our way to the sacred."

~Mark Nepo

"Healing for Younger Self",
"Why I Birthed My Business"

Unconditional Love

"If I were asked to define Motherhood, I would have defined it as
Love in its purest form. Unconditional Love."
~ Revathi Sankaran

"Coming Home",
"Unconditional Love"

Unification

"Of all the frictional resistances, the one that most retards human movement is ignorance, what Buddha called 'the greatest evil in the world.' The friction which results from ignorance ... can be reduced only by the spread of knowledge and the unification of the heterogeneous elements of humanity. No effort could be better spent."
~Nikola Tesla

"Collaboration over Competition"

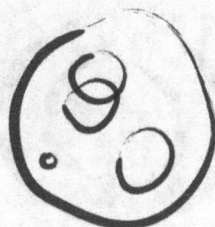

Universe

"There are no extra pieces in the universe. Everyone is here because he or she has a place to fill, and every piece must fit itself into the big jigsaw puzzle."

~Deepak Chopra

"Meditation – It's all about the Cake",
"Trust the Connection",
"Passageways",
"How I became 'Great Moon Heart'",
"Van Gogh",
"Coming Home",
"A Gift From Beyond the Veil",
"The Kingfisher",
"Why I Birthed My Business"

Universal Energy

"Universal Energy is the basis of our entire existence. The warmth of the sun that heats our bodies, the gas we use in our car, the electricity used in the household, are in fact forms of the same energy."
~learningmind.com

"Finding God on the Cricket Pitch",
"Why I Birthed My Business"

Validation

"When you can't let it go, validate it!"
-Jodi Aman

"Signposts for Life",
"The Truth Behind the Clouds"

Values

"Your beliefs become your thoughts,
Your thoughts become your words,
Your words become your actions,
Your actions become your habits,
Your habits become your values,
Your values become your destiny."
~Gandhi

"The Creative Block",
"Connection Within: Refuge in the Body",
"Living Buddhas",
"The Kingfisher"

Vedas

"The basis of Vedic religion contains songs, philosophy and ritual."
~Jennifer Nurick

"Modern Blessing of Ancient Wisdom"

Vibration

"If you want to find the secrets of the universe,
think in terms of energy, frequency and vibration."
~Nikola Tesla

"Wait for the Miracle",
"Humble Mentorship",
"Why I Birthed My Business"

Visualisation

"Visualization is daydreaming with a purpose."
~Bo Bennett

"I See Hearts",
"Van Gogh"

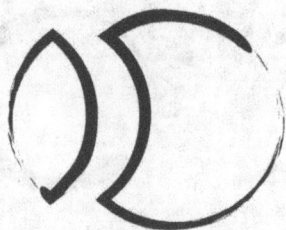

Void

"I need not to be afraid of the void. The void is part of my person.
I need to enter consciously into it. To try to escape from it is to
try to live a lie. It is also to cease to be. My acceptance of despair
and emptiness constitutes my being; to have the courage to
accept despair is to be."
~Michael Novak, The Experience of Nothingness

"Finding God on the Cricket Pitch"

Writing

"Good writing is like a windowpane."
~George Orwell

"Energy of Synchronicity",
"I See Hearts",
"Signposts for Life"

The Universal Conscious Community

Acknowledgements

We acknowledge the land and its traditional custodians, where our stories have originated and / or our life experiences took place.

Big thank you to:

- the International Energetic Healing Association (IEHA) for its dedication to nurturing, enriching and inspiring individuals and communities for over 20 years
- IEHA mentors for their kindness, guidance and support:

  o Martine Negro

  o Jenny Fitzgerald

  o Robyn Vincent

  o Jeanette Young

- IEHA Energy Team of 2018-2019 for holding the space during the renewal phase of the organisation
- the participants of the Energetic Mentoring online event on 18th June 2019, where the energy of the 'Ways to Connect' first presented itself:

  o Simonne Lee

  o Corinne Dosoruth

  o Siina McCallum

  o Irina Gladushchenko

- Class 2019 at the Energetic Health Diploma at Nature Care College for helping to hold the energy of this initiative
- IEHA Energy Team 2019 members for stepping forward and

offering their services to the conscious community. This project would not be possible without their loving support and encouragement every step of the way, and their leadership qualities:

- o Jennifer Nurick
- o Elese Barrymore
- o Elle Reynolds
- 'Unfolding Journeys: Ways to Connect' book custodian Jane Woods for believing in this project's success, her loving care, and for writing an incredibly welcoming foreword for our book
- IEHA 2020 Leadership Team members for applying their versatile skills and offering energetic support to this project:
  - o Jennifer Nurick
  - o Elese Barrymore
  - o Elle Reynolds
  - o Sheila Fawns
  - o Martine Negro
  - o Maxine Pagliasso
  - o Jenny Fitzgerald
- Jenny Fitzgerald for taking on the challenge of becoming the internal editor / author mentor and her dedication to the project, outstanding communication skills and consistency and quality of works delivered
- Nastia Gladushchenko for stepping forward and artistically engaging with the energy of this book as a whole, birthing the cover and subsequent images, colours and brand development
- Tanya Pisk, administrator extraordinaire, for her enthusiasm and love for humans and their journeys and for her incredible skill of extracting keywords that define the current human condition and new ways to connect
- Jennifer Nurick, IEHA president, for her exceptional talent to

find the right words, her willingness to undertake and skillfully lead a research project that brings all the stories in this book together, her time and stress management skills and for leading the organisation by example

- the team of soulful researchers, who developed the 'New Ways to Connect Glossary' for this book, the backbone holding all the stories together, tremendous gratitude for your insight and dedication:

  o Jennifer Nurick
  o Anastasia Giovanoglou
  o Laura Hamblyn
  o Kristy Ismay
  o Elle Reynolds
  o Luca Orlandi
  o Jane Woods

- Irina Gladushchenko for her dedicated service to the light and to all lightworkers. For her commitment to the principles of the IEHA, and for being its custodian for two years. Irina has been the artist holding the many brushes for this project: Mixing the paints, maintaining the vision, and changing the vision with grace as the energy moved. This book is a gift and credit to her commitment and generosity to the light and those on a conscious journey. Thank you for your commitment, presence, generous teaching, wise counsel and grounded action; a true embodiment of spirit on earth

- Our publisher Andrew Akratos and The OMNE Group team, for guiding and educating us so skillfully and generously and providing an excellent service

- Teresa Goudie, the OMNE Group editor, for quality assuring the highest possible writing standards, her patience, openness and kindness

- IEHA insurance partner, Insurance Made Easy (IME) brokers

and its founder James Gillard, and IEHA account manager Philip Watson, for believing in and supporting this project

- our friends at SoulAdvisor, the global facilitator of health and wellness through access, education and advancement of Traditional and Complementary Medicine (T&CM), your encouragement and support were deeply appreciated
- Andrew Johnston who donated his entire library as a gift to this project
- most importantly, the 52 authors who shared their connected stories, nurturing, enriching and inspiring the IEHA community and beyond
- the universe for inviting us all to connect and co-create at this point in time and space, so this book could become a reality

Authors

Andrew Head
"Waiting for Love"
I am the eldest of four siblings. Notable exploits include completing the HSC, travelling overseas to visit family and friends, being part of a crew sailing a tall ship, and all while being blind!
E: andrew.head2015@icloud.com
T: andrewhead21

Amy Morse
"Embracing Resilience"
"Van Gogh"
It's been wonderful sharing my writing in this anthology. I'm also featured in a book called Hope. I aspire to continue writing my fictional novel with themes of love, hurt, betrayal and friendship.
F: Amy Williams (Morse)
I: @Literary_amy

Anastasia Giovanoglou
"Wait for the Miracle"
Core Team Member
Ways to Connect Glossary
I am a glass half full, eternal optimist and see good in everyone.
W: www.genesisofhealth.com.au E: info@genesisofhealth.com.au M: 0402 304 317
F: genesisofhealth
I: @genesisofhealth

Aurélie Hervet
"Unconditional Love"
I am a compassionate human being, lover of life, who is taking every life experience as learning to love, observing, breathing and expressing my feelings.
W: aureliehervet.com
E: aurelie.hervet@gmail.com
I: @aurelie_hervet

Avanti Singh
"Why I Birthed My Business"
I am a Holistic Psychologist, Chopra
Centre Meditation Instructor and
Ayurvedic Practitioner but feel more
a teacher of Modern Mysticism. I use
the integration of ancient wisdom and
modern science to awaken people to
the freedom of unity consciousness.
W: www.mypranaportal.com
E: avanti@mypranaportal.com.au

Carmel Glenane BA Dip Ed.
"Finding 'The Mother'"
I am the embodiment of the 'Language
of The One Heart' through 'Awakening
my
Heart's Intelligence'.
W: www.carmelglenane.com
W: www.atlantis-rising.com.au
E: carmel@carmelglenane.com
F: carmel.glenane
F: carmelglenaneauthor
ONLINE TRAINING HUB: https://
theatlantisrisingmysteryschool.
newzenler.com

Christian Roth
"The Three Ducks"
I am a traveller who is constantly
amazed by the interconnectedness of
all things.
E: christianhjroth@gmail.com

Coco Elder
"Follow Your Heart"
I am an artist and teacher of art and
yoga, seeking to inspire others to
embrace the beauty of nature and life
and live in harmony and love.
W: www.cocoelder.com.au
E: elder.coco8@gmail.com
F: Coco Elder
I: @coco_elder

Corinne Dosoruth
"Life Goes on"
"Energy of Synchronicity"
I like to give people hope.
W: www.backtowellness.life
E: meditation.yoga.healing@gmail.com
F: meditationryde
I: @meditation_peaceful_life

Deborah Shepherd
"The Breath"
As CEO of SoulAdvisor - Australia
and New Zealand, whenever I am
faced with what my next step should
be - gratitude, compassion and joy have
always steered me in the right direction.
E: deborah@souladvisor.com
L: deborahjoyshepherd

Debra Fidler
"A Story of Hope"
"Sisters"
My mission is to help women find their
voice, connect to their passion and
purpose, to awaken the power within.
Vanamali is the spiritual name I was
given by my spiritual teacher. May you
be blessed on this journey we call life.
W: www.debrafidler.com.au
E: connect@debrafidler.com.au
F: VanamaIiDebraFidler
I: @debralfidler

Elain Younn
"Living Buddhas"
As a founder of SoulAdvisor, I believe
that the most important thing we need
to do in life can be done effortlessly and
that a smile can be a miracle.
E: elain@souladvisor.com

Elle Reynolds
"Connection Within: Refuge in the Body"
Ways to Connect Glossary
Core Team Member
I'm a registered counsellor and healer practising on the Sunshine Coast and internationally to support people to deepen into soul, and integrate logic with intuition.
W: centreforholisticliving.com.au
E: elle@centreforholisticliving.com.au
F: centre.for.holistic.living
I: @centre.for.holistic.living

Elese Barrymore
How I became 'Great Moon Heart'
Core Team Member
As an intuitive and empathetic healer, my passion is to help others achieve balance, develop their intuition and have more "felt" life experiences.
W: www.chakrahealingsydney.com.au
E: elese@chakrahealingsydney
M: + 61 416 550 523
F: chakrahealingsydney
I: @chakrahealingsydney

Emma Taylor
"The Phoenix"
I am a passionate holistic kinesiologist and mind body medicine practitioner who is a walking advocate of the profoundly powerful effects of energetic healing. I am inspired to ignite hope within others that change is possible, and that it starts from within.
W: www.emmataylorkinesiology.com.au
F: @emmataylorkinesiology
I: @emmataylor_kinesiology

Etty Ayalon
"Shadow"
I am the daughter of Spirit, I carry the flame of the light bearer and am here to preserve, anchor and share the energy of light, colour, sound and love.
E: ettyayalon@hotmail.com
F: https://www.facebook.com/etty.ayalon

Eva Tiborcz
"The Creative Block"
Variable surrealism is my visual
language, changing, growing,
innovating, hence moving constantly.
E: sterlich2009@hotmail.com
F: Eva Tcz. Sterlich
I: @Sterlich
P: Eva Tcz. Sterlich

Helen Penemenos
"The Truth Behind the Clouds"
Being a wellness practitioner has put
me on an incredible journey.
Combining Reiki, yoga, meditation
and other holistic therapies, I teach
people to live a minimal toxic life and
become independent in their health
care.
My catch-phrase is: "Love of self begins
with self-care".
E: helen@helenarosewellness.com
M: +61 402 286 042

Irina Gladushchenko
"Teacher Aniri"
"Humble Mentorship"
Project Manager
Human ability to transition from
discomfort towards self-mastery has
always inspired me. At present, I am
serving as Director, co-Creation of
the International Energetic Healing
Association (IEHA).
E: mindyourcolour@gmail.com
F: Irina Gladushchenko
I: @irinagladushchenko
L: Irina Gladushchenko

Izabella Jokinen
"Coming Home"
I am an avid traveller, lover of
nature, art, yoga and healthy living.
My husband and I own a wholesale
business through which we import and
create uplifting products that are sold
to retailers across Australia and NZ.
We also run a small guest retreat in
Bellingen, NSW – The Tiny Hideaway.
W: www.elanorawholesale.com.au
E: iz@elanorawholesale.com.au
I: elanora_australia

Izumi Amauchi
"Healing for Younger Self"
My motto is every breath, every step I
take, I live in the vortex of divinity.
W: innercompasshouse.com.au
E: trueself4truehealth@gmail.com

Jacquelyn Bushell
"Desert Dawn"
I invite reconnection with the divine
feminine, nature and the sacred in all
life through storytelling, earth spirit
wisdom and transformational healing.
W: www.sacredpresence.com.au
E: jacquibushell@me.com
F: jacqui.bushell.52
I: @jacqui_bushell_sacredpresence

James Gillard
"Lessons learnt Along the Way"
Passionate about helping my clients to
create the right insurance solutions.
W: www.imeinsurance.com.au
E: jamesg@imeinsurance.com.au

Jane Woods
Foreword
*"Allowing Adversity to Create Good
Change"*
"A Question or Two"
Book Custodian
Proofread
Ways to Connect Glossary
1m another person, just like all of
you. I believe in being true to who I
am.
E: Jane@woods5.com

Jennifer Nurick
"'Landing' with Love"
"Whale Story"
Ways to Connect Glossary
A to Z of the Current Human
Condition
Natural Therapies
Core Team Member
Project Lead
Proofread
I'm an energetic healer, psychotherapist, mother, wife and daughter. Lover of life and nature.
W: www.jennynurick.com
E: info@jennynurick.com
I: @psychotherapy.central
I: @goldenwomancentre

Jenny Fitzgerald
"Darkness to Light"
Core Team Member
Internal Editorials
I'm a transformation life coach who helps people find freedom from anxiety through self-awareness and forgiveness.
W: www.jennyfitzgerald.com.au
E: jenny@jennyfitzgerald.com.au

Joan Lewis
"Passageways"
I am a follower of the teachings of many spiritual leaders who acknowledge the bridge between science and ancient wisdoms...
My human story is one of transition, growth, curiosity, and evolution to build a foundation of wisdom.
E: missztree@gmail.com

Julia Pomazkina
"Modern Blessing of Ancient Wisdom"
I am an Ayurvedic practitioner and herbalist – offering health consultations, herbal programs, a range of ayurvedic therapies and energy healing sessions.
I specialize in female health, endocrine and autoimmune disorders, chronic fatigue, digestive health, stress and anxiety management and general vitality and rejuvenation.
W: www.sunriseayurveda.com.au
F: SunriseAyurvedaAustralia
P: +612 8003 4601

Kate Baker
"The Kingfisher"
I see my photography and my life as an alchemical journey of connection.
W: www.katejbaker.com
E: kate@katejbaker.com
F: katejbaker
I: @katejbaker

Kristy Ismay
"Fairies, Readings and Spirit Guides Whispers"
Ways to Connect Glossary
Core Team Member
I am an intuitive energy healer and he IEHA global accreditations manager. Mother of three amazing boys. Founder of 'Freedom Flow Healing'.
W: inspiredwildandfree.com/energy-healing
E: kgirl_ismay@hotmail.com
I: @freedom_flow_healing

Lily C Dodd
"Born to See"
Allowing the desires of my heart to take form and become a reality as I focus on staying true to my life's purpose!
B: Lily C Dodd Digital Publisher
W: https://www.whollynatural.net
E: info@whollynatural.net
F: http://www.facebook.com/whollynatural
I: @whollynatural

Lisa Cohen
"The Essence of My Heart"
I am a mother, healer, partner, friend, daughter, sister, wild woman and creative living in Sydney.
W: www.in2balancekinesiology.com.au
E: lisa@in2balancekinesiology.com.au
F: in2balancekinesiology
I: @in2balance_kinesiology

Luca Orlandi
"Trust the Connection"
Ways to Connect Glossary
Core Team Member
I believe that crystal intelligence and the language of colours is a gateway enabling every one of us to remember and reconnect with the infinite wisdom that exists within.
W: www.yntoyou.com.au
W: www.ynotcrystals.com
F: ynotyouaustralia
I: @ynot.you

Luke Myers
"For the Love of Passion"
Losing everything can be an opportunity to start again as a better version of you.
E: lukeamyers@hotmail.com

Marilyn McMullen
"Meditation – It's all about the Cake"
In Loving Memory

Martine Negro
"The Power of Tuning in"
Core Team Member
I assist people all over the world as an energy mentor to achieve long term well-being through living authentically.
Co-founder and life member of the IEHA Senior trainer at Nature College, Sydney
Conference speaker
Author of "Hacking the Well-Being Code through Energetic Intelligence".
W: www.martinenegro.com

Maxine Pagliasso
"She Listens Still"
"Energy of Synchronicity"
Core Team Member
I am a teacher, an energy healer and a strong empath who finds beauty in everything.
E: earthstarenergyhealing@gmail.com
I: @earth_star_energy_healing

Mel Rourke
"I See Hearts"
Friends describe me as being a kind, creative soul who is here to inspire others to honour their true authenticity and connect them back to their heart and unlimited abundance within.
W: www.lifeenergetichealing.com.au
E: hello@lifeenergetichealing.com.au
I: @lifeenergetichealing

Nastia Gladushchenko
"Collaboration over Competition"
Core Team Member
Book Cover Design
Illustrations
My work looks at the relationship between humans and the plant world and aims to mimic the temporal and playful nature of plants through dreamy tones and organic forms. As well as running a personal art practice, I'm interested in creating pieces for and with the community to allow them to access art and to experience its benefits in public spaces.
W: www.nastia-gladushchenko.com
E: nastia.gladushchenko@gmail.com
I: @nastiagladu

Nina Maudslay
"The Song of Healing"
I am passionate about all things birth-related especially the wellbeing of women
and mothers. I believe that great community support can allow women to thrive,
living and mothering with confidence, awareness, compassion and self-care.
E: bloomflourish@gmail.com
M: 0423261186
F: @bloomandflourish

Authors

Norah Lynn Copithorne
"A Conscious Path"
I'm Canadian-born and have had a wandering life that's allowed me to live in many different countries. Arrived in Australia many years ago where I worked a variety of jobs in technology. These days I'm a 'Conscious Lens' and mentor.
E: copithorne.97@gmail.com
M: +61452218369
F: A Conscious Lens
S: norah.copithorne

Robyn Vincent
"Dance of Life"
I have been a spiritual healer, taught dance, energetic healing, reflexology and spiritual teachings on rays and initiations, founded and established Energetic Healing Association.
E: vincent.robyn@gmail.com
M: +61434 293 359

Sandra O'Brien
"A Turning Point"
I have found life very difficult at times, but in reflection, it's all being worthwhile, and I wouldn't change anything.
E: Obrien.sandra57@gmail.com

Sharmini Weerasinghe
"Food for the Soul, Body, and Mind"
I enjoy connecting to people and to contribute to a collective community for the betterment of all.
E: email ncsw@ozemail.com.au

Sheila Fawns
"Signposts for Life"
"A Little Divine Intervention"
"Temper Tantrums"
Core Team Member
I am a holistic coach and psychotherapist passionate about helping people get the very best out of themselves, understand and release underlying patterns and dynamics which may be making their lives difficult or limiting them.
I currently run regular groups and classes on wellness, meditation, mindfulness, self-empowerment, women's circles, relationship building and energy healing as well as one-to-one sessions.
E: sheila.fawns@gmail.com
M: 0418 693 561

Simonne Lee
"Who Said That?"
I am a coach, clinical hypnotherapist, energy alchemist & animal communicator. Everything is all about our energy and how you're holding it.
W: www.simonneleemethod.com
E: hello@simonnelee.com
F: simonneleeofficial

Summer Cowie
"Taking Responsibility for Your Own Life"
I am a 21-year-old free-spirit living and learning on the Sunshine Coast.
I: @Summerirelandd

Susie Nelson-Smith
"A Gift From Beyond the Veil"
I love life and all of its mysteries . . .
W: www.crystalsoundandlight.com
E: karyna@crystalsoundandlight.com

Tanya Pisk
Ways to Connect Glossary
A to Z of the Current Human
Condition
Core Team Member
I am a support coordinator. I enjoy
helping people to explore their spiritual
selves and connect with providers in
the community to meet their goals.
W: auscaresupport.com.au
E: tanya.pisk@auscaresupport.com.au
P: 1800 940 515

Vasu Devi Laura Hamblyn
"Finding God on the Cricket Pitch"

Ways to Connect Glossary
Core Team Member
I live in the UK, in a large town north
of London, I am devoted to my
spiritual path, and I've discovered that
real joy comes from service, I am a
qualified healer and therapist,
meditation teacher, a vegan chef, and a
solo mother to a wonderful boy.
E: vasudevishanti@gmail.com
F: Laura VasuDevi @
meditationsandhealings
I: vasudevi_laurah

Yia Alias
"Bone Woman – Shamanic Mystic"
I am a transpersonal counsellor
women's mystery teacher offering
healing through ritual, supporting
women through life's transitional
thresholds.
W: www.yiaalias.com
E: yiaalias@gmail.com

Yukari Doi
"I Followed my Dreams"
I am a healer who follows my dreams
and my heart.
E: yukari.doi58@gmail.com
F: https://www.facebook.com/yukari.
doi1

Organisations

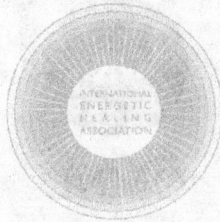

International Energetic Healing Association (IEHA)

International Energetic Healing Association (IEHA) is a governing body to provide services to natural therapies practitioners world-wide.

As a 'Universal Conscious Community', our mission is to become the respected voice of energetic healing worldwide, and our goal is to nurture, enrich and inspire all beings to live empowered lives. Our focus is on the wellbeing, joy and inner peace for all our practitioners and their clients, providing them with the support, education and assistance for them to run their businesses with all their natural therapies modalities, including energetic healing.

W: www.internationaleha.org

E: cocreation@internationaleha.org

F: InternationalEHA

I: @ international_eha

OMNE

At OMNE, our mission is to empower inspirational authors to succeed.

Whether you're looking for guidance to help you self-publish or a complete done-for-you publishing solution, we have the answer to all your needs.

W: www.omne.com.au

E: info@omne.com.au

P: + 61 2 8005 7370

SoulAdvisor

SoulAdvisor

Our purpose is to be a global facilitator of health and wellness through access, education and advancement of Traditional and Complementary Medicine (T&CM).

W: www.souladvisor.com

F: souladvisors

I: @_souladvisor

L: www.linkedin.com/company/souladvisor

INSURANCE MADE EASY

BROKERS SINCE 1992

Insurance Made Easy (IME)

IME is a trusted insurance broker who specialises in the natural therapies insurance market for Australian practitioners, servicing Australia-wide with expertise in risk management, allied health insurance (professional indemnity) public liability, product liability, and commercial property cover.

W: www.imeinsurance.com.au

E: pwatson@imeinsurance.com.au

Complementary Therapies

There are many forms of healing and, depending on the modality, each session will vary as every practitioner is unique in what they offer in a session.

Most sessions are interactive with the client either laying on a massage table or sitting on a chair. The practitioner utilises a range of methods, tools and techniques relevant to specific modalities. The session can be face-to-face, remote or distant, all designed to uncover the root cause of their ailment and bring the client back into alignment and balance.

~Anastasia Giovanoglou

There are 600+ various modalities, but in this book we are introducing those mentioned by the authors.

1. Acupuncture

"Acupuncture is probably the best-known practice associated with traditional Chinese medicine (TCM) and involves inserting very fine needles at key points on the body. These needles may be rotated by the practitioner, heated, or have a mild electric current applied to them."

~ www.souladvisor.com

2. Animal Communication

"Most of us already communicate with our pets; we watch their behaviour and are able to read their body language, sounds and even get a feeling of what's going on for them. Animal Communication takes it that step further. Through Animal Communication, Simonne is able to communicate with your pet in a free-flowing conversation. The method that Simonne uses is through a deep connection using the five senses as the process of communicating simultaneously. Simonne is able to exchange feelings, sensations, tastes, smells, thoughts, images and what she calls 'short movies' of their experiences."

~ www.simonnelee.com/

3. Aura-Soma

"Harnessing the vibrational powers of Mother Nature, Aura-Soma is a system of colour, plant and crystal energies that enhance happiness and vitality. Created using the highest quality organic and biodynamic ingredients, our products bring ease, balance and calm to your energetic system. While strengthening and protecting the aura, they empower and elevate."

~ www.aura-soma.com

4. Ayurveda

"Ancient medicinal tradition based on Vedic scriptures, aiming to alleviate human suffering by promoting health and treating disease – physically, mentally, emotionally and spiritually – through correct living, eating, physical and spiritual practices and herbal medicines."

~ www.sunriseayurveda.com.au

5. Ayurvedic massage

"Therapeutic body oiliation massage with warm ayurvedic herbal oils chosen specifically to the patient's constitution and health conditions, either as a standalone treatment or as an integral part of ayurvedic panchakarma detoxification program."

~ www.sunriseayurveda.com.au

6. Basecamp Retreat

"A base camp in the remote location, from which to experience the wilderness and explore desert spirituality alone and in community."

~ www.kooraretreat.com.au

7. Chakra Balance

"Chakra Balancing refers to aligning the seven major chakras that make up the Energy System – the base chakra, sacral chakra, solar plexus chakra, heart chakra, throat chakra, third eye, and crown chakra."

~ www.chakrahealingsydney.com.au

8. Colour Therapy

"'The Secret Language of Colour' is your key to unlocking the extraordinary healing power of colour, how colour can affect and influence our mood and emotions and evoke reactions, and it is used in medicine and for healing as colour therapy."

~ www.innasegal.com

9. Community Nursing

"In partnership with their local communities, nurses in community health work to prevent illness and promote health across the lifespan by identifying barriers to healthy lifestyles and general wellness. They work with families and communities to empower individuals accessing care to change unhealthy lifestyles and provide post-acute care to people in their homes."

~ www.apna.asn.au

10. Counselling

"Counselling involves talking with a suitably trained professional about concerns or difficulties you are facing, and receiving support from them to help you improve your mental, emotional and possibly physical wellbeing. Categorised as a talk-based therapy, counselling is intended to help you gain clarity and understanding of the challenges you face in a confidential and non-judgemental setting."

~ www.souladvisor.com

11. Crystal Intelligence

"Crystals have been utilised by mankind for thousands of years, and loving them is not hard to do. We admire their looks, colours and shapes. Also, crystals can be an invaluable tool in our life's journey."

~ www.ynotcrystals.com

12. Crystal Therapy

"Crystal therapy is a traditional modality based on the idea that various semi-precious minerals have unique abilities to gather or focus subtle forms of energy that can promote wellbeing. By keeping crystals near you in the form of jewellery, placing them on your body during a therapy session, or by positioning them around your home, many people believe they can recharge and harmonise the body's energy field."

~ www.souladvisor.com

13. Energetic Mentoring

"Selected energetic tools (NLP, TFT/EFT, Dowsing, Imagery, deep energetic meditation and imagery work) are used during the session. As true healing comes from within, you will be engaging in an internal exploration of what is primarily interfering with your health; you will be guided by your own intuitive wisdom to return to your authentic self while discovering the hidden message behind your symptom, bringing the natural flow of your energy back to find its own balance."

~ www.martinenegro.com

14. Energetic Healing

"Using various energetic tools and methods to assist a recipient in reconnecting to their body and their healing ability, so they can feel their energy and take control of their wellbeing."

~ www.internationaleha.org

15. Flower Essences

"The use of flower essences have gained worldwide recognition due to their contribution to holistic health and emotional healing. However, these subtle medicines can become somewhat 'watered-down' as they are difficult to study on a biochemical level due to the limitations of science and research. Although this shouldn't mean we ignore the thousands of years they have been used traditionally to heal physical and mental imbalances."

~ www.endeavour.edu.au

16. 'Ignite your Spirit' (IYS)

"'Ignite Your Spirit' is a form of spiritual counselling which practically and sensitively assists people to release blocks in their mind, body and energy field which are causing limitation or frustration."

~ www.shantimission.org

17. Indigenous Healing

"As the world begins to rediscover the wisdom of traditional healing modalities, the shortfalls of Western medicine are becoming increasingly obvious. The UN Declaration on the Rights of Indigenous Peoples specifically mentions that traditional cultures are entitled 'to maintain their health practices'".

~ www.souladvisor.com

18. Kinesiology

"Kinesiology is a holistic modality which uses muscle monitoring to identify and assess any stress and imbalances within the body, on a physical, emotional, mental and spiritual level to bring the body back to homeostasis."

~ www.genesisofhealth.com.au

19. Matrix Reimprinting

"It is a modality created by Karl Dawson using EFT (Emotional Freedom Technique) to change core beliefs to achieve one's desired life."

~ www.innercompasshouse.com.au

20. Meditation

"Meditation is a very broad term that encompasses diverse practices whose common goal is to develop a peaceful, serene state of mind and clarity of thought. There are so many different styles and varieties of meditation that classifying them can be a difficult task. One approach involves grouping them according to practices that have a spiritual basis or goal, techniques that involve concentrating your attention on a particular subject, and methods that involve observation of the present moment."

~ www.souladvisor.com

21. Past Lives

"Past life regression is a method that uses hypnosis to recover what practitioners believe are memories of past lives or incarnations. The practice is widely considered discredited and unscientific by medical practitioners, and experts generally regard claims of recovered memories of past lives as fantasies or delusions or a type of confabulation."

~ www.wikipedia.org

22. Pranic Healing

"Pranic Healing is the use of Prana, the natural life energy, to create health, vitality and prosperity. The modern practice of Pranic Healing was established by Choa Kok Sui, a Filipino scientist, chemical engineer and enlightened teacher."

~ www.pranichealing.com.au

23. Psychic Reading

"A psychic reading is a specific attempt to discern information through the use of heightened perceptive abilities; or natural extensions of the basic human senses of sight, sound, touch, taste and instinct. These natural extensions are claimed to be clairvoyance (vision), clairsentience (feeling), claircognisance (factual knowing) and clairaudience (hearing) and the resulting statements made during such an attempt."

~ www.wikipedia.org

24. Psycho-Spiritual Training

"Psychospiritual is a term used for the integration of the psychological and the spiritual, usually heard in psychology and religion, a supplementation of the two fields."

~ www.trueisense.com

25. Reiki

"Reiki is non-invasive modality based on the idea of a practitioner intentionally channelling universal energy to support their patient's physical and emotional healing. The practitioner focuses energy through their hands, placing them on or just above the person being treated. Unlike some energy modalities in which the practitioner endeavours to actively intervene with blockages in a person's energy, Reiki is intended to encourage and stimulate a person's innate powers of self-healing, and help them re-establish their own internal control over their energy balance."

~ www.souladvisor.com

26. Satsang

"Satsang / satsaṅga / satsangam is a word which comes from Sanskrit, meaning to associate with true people, or to be in the company of true people. It is also related to sitting with a sat guru, or in a group meeting seeking that association."

~ www.wikipedia.org

27. Sound Therapy

"The use of sound as a path towards healing and transformation predates written records and is common to most ancient cultures. The didgeridoo played by Indigenous Australians, the shamanic drumming of Native Americans, the mantras that are an intrinsic part of Indian tradition, and the hymns and prayers in Western religion, are all examples of combining sound with spirituality. From these origins, sound therapy has evolved into a contemporary healing modality with specialisations such as music therapy and clinical treatments for tinnitus and pain relief."

~ www.souladvisor.com

28. Transpersonal Therapy

"As with most variations of talk therapy, transpersonal therapy has the power to improve a person's view of life and increase their confidence in themselves. It can help the person heal from a variety of events as well as encourage positive body-mind relations to improve the overall quality of life. Transpersonal therapy takes a holistic approach to talk therapy by focusing not only on the mind but the wellness of the spirit. It hones in on the physical, mental, social, emotional, creative, and intellectual needs of the individual. This personalised approach facilitates healing and growth for a happier and healthier adult."

~ www.betterhelp.com

29. Workshops

"Workshops are typically short educational courses that focus on specific concepts in a particular course of study, or on the development of a particular skill.

Workshops are often informal and interactive. Trainers and participants may take part in discussions, presentations, debates, or hands-on demonstrations to engage with new ideas and techniques."

~ www.goodtherapy.org

30. Yoga

"In the Western world, yoga is most popularly known as a type of exercise focusing on postures and relaxation techniques that aid in stress relief and flexibility. However, the physical poses associated with yoga are only one aspect of a greater collection of practices originally developed with the intention of enriching the body, mind and spirit."

~ www.souladvisor.com

A to Z of the
Current Human Condition

www.ingramcontent.com/pod-product-compliance
Lightning Source LLC
Chambersburg PA
CBHW011829020426
42334CB00027B/2984